AUSPICIOUS

EMBRACING THE PATH TOWARD COURAGE, CONVICTION AND CONFIDENCE

AUSPICIOUS

EMBRACING THE PATH TOWARD COURAGE, CONVICTION AND CONFIDENCE

REETU GUPTA

AUSPICIOUS

Published in 2023 by Dolce Media Group Inc.
Dolce Media Group Inc.
111 Zenway Blvd., Suite 30, Vaughan, Ont. L4H 3H9
T: (905) 264-6789
www.dolcemedia.ca

Publisher's Note

The opinions expressed in this book are those of the author(s) and do not necessarily reflect the views of the publisher. Although all efforts have been made to ensure accuracy of this work, Dolce Media Group Inc. does not assume liability for content, accuracy of dates, places, names and citations. This book is a work of nonfiction. No liability is assumed with respect to the use of the information and advice contained herein are not meant to substitute for the advice of your family's physician or other trained healthcare professionals. You are advised to consult with healthcare professionals with regard to all matters pertaining to you and your family's health and well-being.

ISBN NUMBER 978-0-9881192-7-7

Printed in Canada

To my parents,
Dr. Steve Gupta and Mrs. Rashmi Gupta,
who love me unconditionally.

And to my brother, Suraj, and my sisters,
Reema and Shelley, who support me endlessly.
This book is for you.

You are all the lanterns that light my path,
that keep me glowing so that I can continue to share
and spread my love to those who walk this
soul-filled path with me.

CONTENTS

PROLOGUE

"Face Everything and Rise."

— Reetu Gupta

AUSPICIOUS: PROMISING; ADVANTAGEOUS; WELL-TIMED

As you hold this book in your hand or on an e-reader, or if you are listening to it as an audio book, know that by the very act of doing so, you are doing something beautiful for yourself. You have made the decision to be open to change, to be open to knowledge and to growth. I am with you every step of the way on this journey.

I am also incredibly grateful that you have chosen this book, and my deepest wish is that it brings you love, happiness and a deep inner sense of serenity and peacefulness. Maybe you chose this book for a specific reason and maybe, out of all the myriad titles available, something in your soul stirred as you picked up my book. A small voice told you that this is an auspicious moment for you, one which the Universe is guiding you toward.

So what does the word "auspicious" actually mean?

Its formal definition is when a moment or an opportunity is auspicious, it is conducive to success, either in the moment or in the future. And so, by picking up this book, *Auspicious: Embracing the Path Toward Courage, Conviction and Confidence*, your heart is telling you that you are ready to receive the messages I am sharing with you within these pages. As you manifest these practices in your daily life, you will be guided along your own unique path so that you can actualize *your* soul purpose, one that is unique to you — because there is *only one you.* You were born in a specific place at a specific moment in time; you are here for a purpose that only you can fulfil.

No matter the reason, the hand of destiny has inspired you to choose this book as a means of honouring your dreams and making a remarkable life-changing connection to the Divine Universe, a decision that will fill your life with daily bursts of gratitude, affirmative habits, actualizing dreams, fear-busting confidence and acceptance, all viable and positive spiritual tools to facilitate and effect transformative and open-minded change. Many choose to write about negative experiences in life and create bonds with others that are based solely on negative circumstances. My intentions, however, are to create a love-filled space where together you and I can share positive experiences and joyful adventures, so that we can all move forward with a playful and loving spirit.

As such, I have included many of the ways in which I greet each day with a positive and grateful attitude. I have also shared within these pages some of the ways that I have learned to listen to my intuition, that soft supportive voice that comes from the heart and guides us to how we can best handle life's challenges and ultimately bless these struggles.

In his book *The Alchemist* (Harper One; Trade Paperback Edition, 2008, translated by Alan R. Clarke), Brazilian author Paulo Coelho tells us that the voice of our heart is, in fact, the voice of the Divine Universe guiding us forward in love and light. It is the voice that always has our back, encourages us to believe in ourselves, follow our dreams and celebrate our purpose on this Earth — one that is uniquely and singularly tailored to each one of us. It is also the voice that lights our journey as we actualize our soul purpose on this Earth.

From my earliest recall I have clear memories of what I wanted and what it was I sought in order to become the most auspicious, authentic version of myself.

As a young girl, my mother and my father taught me — in fact, instilled in me — these values. My mother, Rashmi, encouraged me from an early age to believe in myself, to be comfortable in my own skin and to own who I was at every milestone along the way as I evolved into adulthood.

Both she and my father, Steve, inspired me to speak my mind, to listen to my inner voice, the voice that always whispered to me, "I am, I can, I will."

In fact, at a young age, I knew in my soul that the force that would drive my path forward was one that was, and continues to be, fueled by the three guiding Cs in my life: Courage, Conviction and Confidence.

It is these rock-solid values that, as you make your way through this book, will uplift and empower you, dear readers, to live a life that actualizes your most authentic, auspicious selves. It is a life that will inspire you to live every moment *with* happiness, rather than *for* happiness.

My favourite example of what strength and power look like is symbolized by the great and mighty tiger, an animal that, in many cultures, symbolizes illumination, energy and protection.

It is my symbol, my inner narrative that whispers to me that no challenge and no upset has the ability to change who I am; my authentic self is not compromised by the dark spaces that I have to negotiate my way through. I am strength; I am virtue; I am victory. At that point, the crippling emotion that is fear transforms from the definition of "fear everything and run" to "*face everything and rise.*"

We all have the ability to be tigers, an image that is key to remember when the swirl of life presents itself. We have all had experiences when things aren't going our way and we start saying things like, "Why me? Why did that happen? Why now?" But when we do this, we forget to count our own blessings because usually we are too busy counting someone else's. But when we shift our perspective and honestly look at each challenge, struggle or loss that we go through, we will see that we have learned a host of valuable lessons. When we let go of our pasts and open our minds and our hearts to change, try our best and then surrender the outcome, our faith and trust in the Universe's love and positive intentions will manifest the best possible outcome for us.

It is about dispelling doubt and replacing it with courage, confidence and a belief in self.

And that is where the importance of faith comes in. Having faith that we are exactly where we are meant to be; having faith in our abilities, in the Divine Universe and God or Higher Power of our understanding.

As you travel through the pages and chapters of this book, my wish for you is to embrace and manifest the very definition of an *auspicious* outcome — one that is felicitous, favourable and conducive to success.

Thank you for making this world we live in a better place by the very act of becoming your most auspicious, authentic self, one that embraces the path with courage, conviction, confidence and gratitude.

I am grateful for *you*.

With Love and Light,

Reetu

CHAPTER 1

AUSPICIOUSLY YOURS: CREATING THE PATH TO FULFILLING YOUR AUTHENTIC SOUL PURPOSE

"I will not make a decision that compromises my integrity or values. I am as strong as thunder when it comes to my morals, and I will always stand up and defend what is right for humanity. I am also gentle as a flower with my love and devotion."

— Reetu Gupta

Hello and the warmest of welcomes to you as you embark upon your journey to becoming your most auspicious and authentic self.

Before we start this partnership of self-affirmation and joy, I would like to share with you a little about myself so we can be hand-in-hand travellers as we walk this personal journey together.

My name is Reetu Gupta, and I am a little sister, an older sister, a daughter, a granddaughter, an aunt, a friend, a CEO, a guided meditation teacher, a dancer, a writer and the Ambassadress for my family's company, The Gupta Group. My family's enterprise ventures encompass real estate, hospitality, mining and venture capital, and it is also the parent company to Easton's Group of Hotels (the company that I grew up in and eventually became the

CEO of, leading it to become one of Canada's largest private hotel development firms).

In partnership with my brother, Suraj Gupta, I am also the co-founder and Chief Strategy Officer of Rogue Insight Capital Ltd., the diversification arm for The Gupta Group. Rogue has a global portfolio of private equity and venture capital investments with the mission to provide funds for socially impactful companies that have female, minority or immigrant leadership.

I have been honoured with the distinction of being one of WXN's Top 100 Most Powerful Women in 2020 and 2019 as well as one of Canada's Top 40 Under 40 in June 2017.

In June of 2020, I recreated and launched The Gupta Family Foundation, on which I serve as president and Co-Chair. The principles of our foundation are aligned with the United Nations Sustainable Development Goals, which focus on equality, education and empowerment through satisfying basic needs like food, water, schooling, etc.

Outside of the hospitality and real estate industry, I work as a life coach and mentor to women who are looking for professional, spiritual and life guidance. As the founder and president of the Shakti Society, I donate my time to teaching monthly meditation classes pro bono to empower attendees on their quest to becoming their best possible selves.

I share these facts with you so that you can get a sense of my professional acumen, while at the same time I have to admit that I still have so much I would like to accomplish and so many dreams that I not only hope but also plan to achieve. I am blessed to do what I love, but what is most important to me is that I do not separate my professional self from my spiritual self. I am one with my heart and soul, which is how I choose to celebrate and actualize my most auspicious, authentic self.

When the Universe sent me down to Earth, I was born into the hotel industry with an explosion of passion! My other true passion, my soul purpose, is to make a positive difference, to spread love and happiness into the world; it is my *raison d'être.* It is an appetite with no limits and one that has, and will continue to be, a fundamental building block toward actualizing my purpose in life.

I have truly left no stone unturned on my journey so far, as I walk through life managing and defusing the many challenges and misperceptions that life has presented me with based on my race, my gender identity and my age.

However, let me begin at the beginning, for it is in the everyday victories, triumphs and hardships that we as individuals find life's common experiences, ones that allow us to identify and share one on one, brother to sister, friend to friend and heart to heart.

My love of fashion captured my heart at a very young age. I would collect jewelry as a child, pulling them apart and making new custom pieces; I would take clothes from my mom's closet and re-purpose them into creative and unique outfits. I couldn't sew, however, so I had to cobble the pieces together with tape. I have never cared about being considered "in fashion" because, for me, fashion is how I personally and artistically express myself. It is a statement that is singular to me. Wonderfully, my fashion statements of individuality and independence are ones that my mother, Rashmi, has always supported. When she grew up in India, she did not wear the traditional Indian dress as was the custom. Instead, she would take her father's clothes and also make custom pieces! In fact, fashion is a passion that I pursued as a model in my early 20s and one that you will read about in an upcoming chapter. No matter how "out there" my fashion accessories might have appeared to others, my mother encouraged me to "walk the walk," to not be shy, to show everyone my fashion sense. This was the first time my three Cs whispered to me — that I had the courage, conviction and confidence to express myself.

In fact, these three self-affirming beliefs are my personal

mantras, my goalposts to living my most authentic life — truly my warrior armour when the chips are down. These tenets, Courage, Conviction and Confidence, inspire me and continue to uplift me as I create the path forward to actualizing my own personal destiny. They are what give me the courage to look at myself in the mirror every morning and acknowledge my strengths, while also shoring up my weaknesses. It is from this affirming act of self-love that I then have the confidence to move forward with complete conviction, a state of being that empowers me and allows others to recognize that I am here for a "well-intentioned make-a-difference" purpose, and also that I am open to the Universe's messages, ones that help me help others.

All that being said, and with pure and open-heart disclosure, while it may sound like I have breezed through life to get to this place of peaceful serenity and calm, I have, like you, dealt with many challenges and upsets in my life. But I was determined that I would not only excel despite them but also to celebrate those hardships and triumphs. I do not focus on negative outcomes; rather I am someone who thrives on finding the positives in everything I do. And it is for these reasons that I decided to share with you, esteemed readers, all of whom I am confident are on your own paths to living your best lives, the steps I embraced and the experiences that I encountered on the way to living my most auspicious, authentic, soul-purposeful life.

I am sure that one of your first questions may be "But how do I go about discerning what my true purpose in life is?"

Finding the answer to that question is not an easy task, but it is possible when you do the work and invest your faith in the powerful intentions that the Universe has for each one of us.

We can look back at our past and take an inventory of the decisions we made, the paths that we took to get us "from there to here," but at the same time, it is imperative that we do not get stuck in a state of self-recrimination if our past decisions were less than we'd hoped for today.

I would like to share with you an anecdote that involves my cherished Aunt Carole, who is a much-respected intuitive elder in my life, a loving support who continues to mentor me through both the hundreds of questions I have for her on a continual basis, as well as about the ways in which I can make the most important and significant impacts for those who need the most help in life. It is a search that I believe is the ongoing reason for my soul purpose in my life.

As I mentioned previously, my passion and determination to succeed in life is unbridled, and one that has, at times, a modicum of impatience attached to it. It is at these times that I speak with my Aunt Carole to seek her guidance and knowledge.

My questions can be incessant, and it is at these times that Aunt Carole will say these two things to me:

First: "What do you think *you* should do, Reetu?" which empowers me to reflect and reconsider the options I feel are best suited to the issue.

The second thing that my Aunt Carole continues to tell me on an ongoing basis is "Slow down, Grasshopper, have patience," the latter being a reference to the 1970s television show *Kung Fu* starring David Carradine as Kwai Chang Caine, a Shaolin monk. Caine, a young martial arts student who was often unfocused and distracted, was called "Grasshopper" by the Grand Master, Master Po, as a means of encouraging him to stay focused on his mission of fulfilling his life's purpose. It is a lesson I take to heart on a continuous basis — and Grasshopper is still my nickname today!

Of course, human nature is such that it is hard not to get mired in the many roles we are called upon to fulfil in our daily lives. To be everything to everyone all the time is an impossible demand that we should be aware of as a non-serving energy sucker. As women, we feel this immense pressure "to be all to all."

Traditionally, our roles have always inherently been those of nurturers; we are Mother Nature's conduit as we bring new life into this world. The expectations on us, coupled with the resistance against us, has caused the movement that women have experienced over the past several decades. We have fought for empowerment every step of the way, and although we have seen some success, we are a long way from becoming equal partners and contributors to the well-being of society.

Intriguingly, in Hinduism, our goddesses are revered as having supreme powers. For example, the Goddess Lakshmi represents prosperity and balance; Goddess Durga represents strength; Goddess Parvati represents devotion; and Goddess Radha represents unconditional love.

In the Hindu culture, our gods are also characterized as having multiple arms, each one holding an item that symbolizes a particular virtue, such as courage, wisdom, selfless service, meditation, etc. In fact, Durga, a warrior goddess whose iconography shows her riding a lion or a tiger, has between eight and eighteen hands, each holding a weapon to destroy negativity and create bliss. To me, the underlying meaning of these multiple appendages is that we, as humans, can manage and tackle so much more than we think possible. We don't need eight hands to achieve greatness when our spiritual intentions are such that when we have a strong connection to our heart's messages and we follow its voice, we will be guided on the path to happiness and fulfilment.

What is important to remember, though — a life value that I will remind you of often throughout this book — is that, as we walk this path on a daily basis, we ensure that we live life *with* happiness and not *for* happiness.

I promise you that as you make your way through this book or e-reader that you are holding in your hands or that you are listening to as an audio book, you CAN and WILL be guided to harness the power you have within. You will be equipped with the tools to unleash your inner Devi (Hindi word for goddess) and you will celebrate the journey of living the life that you have always dreamed about achieving.

And just how will you do that?

Let me share a personal experience with you that occurred at a time when I was just beginning my career in the hotel industry. I had been awarded my Bachelor of Business Administration (BBA) from the University of Toronto, with a major in marketing. I was tremendously excited to develop my own personal marketing strategy for Easton's Group of Hotels. I was assigned to a project that was in the pre-launch stage of debuting our first combination hotel and banquet hall endeavour and it was at that point that I quickly realized that the hotel industry was completely dominated by men.

As you can imagine, as a young person fresh out of university and also the boss' daughter, my capabilities were questioned. There was an inherent belief that as the boss' daughter I was appointed to the position rather than having earned it.

Oh my, were they in for a surprise!

My initiative for work does not come from a financial basis but rather from a passion for what I do. Moreover, I watched as my parents worked extremely hard from the time I was little; they came from nothing to achieve great heights. Their powerful example to work hard while being family-centric is a core lesson that I do not take for granted.

And so, when I first began to bring my ideas to the boardroom table, these well-entrenched company men would listen because I was the "boss' daughter," then offer me a symbolic condescending pat on the back, which was meant to say, *OK darling, we will pretend to do it your way.*

But it was clearly obvious that these men did not want to take direction from me, and it left me questioning what my next steps should be. Should I demand that they follow my instructions, which didn't sit right with me, because although I saw myself as an owner of the business, I was uncomfortable making demands and taking advantage of it? I have also been taught to respect my elders and never to be disrespectful, so I chose to be patient.

My approach, my modus operandi, has always been to present with a silent Mona Lisa smile so that people don't know what I'm thinking. Eventually, I decided to let the team try it their way, go down their own path and learn for themselves. Lo and behold, a week later this same team of men came to the follow-up meeting with tasks either not completed or with results in hand that were not feasible. In subsequent meetings that I chaired, the men, albeit reluctantly, agreed to the strategies that I proposed as a way to effectively move forward. Very soon after opening our hotel and banquet undertaking, this new venture became the number one banquet hall in Vaughan, Ontario.

So what did I learn from this challenge?

I learned that the second we start losing faith in ourselves and start believing what others are saying about us is the very second that we lose our conviction and our confidence in ourselves. When we lose our confidence in our abilities, it makes us feel as though the other person has the ability to strip our sense of personal power and empowerment from us. No one, no person, no group can ever take away your personal power.

Remember these three words: Courage, Conviction and Confidence. They are connected to the affirmative traits that you will come across often in this book; ones that will be your markers to becoming your most auspicious self.

What is highly important to state here is the fact that life's challenges come in many forms, and that I do not intend, with any malice, to pass judgment on our male counterparts.

The only way society can move forward is together, all humans of all identities.

Sometimes women try to better their own personal positions at the expense of our female colleagues — a tendency that I fervently hope is now in the rear-view mirror. I will briefly share with you my experience of sitting on the board of a renowned charitable organization.

This board was organizing an event to honour four great Canadian women, an event that I was asked to emcee. As you can imagine, I was honoured and excited — I looked up to the women on this board and I was humbled that I was asked to be a part of the event. I was the youngest by far and the only woman "of colour."

A few days after being asked, I received a phone call from a board member, advising me that certain individuals who were involved in the event were not comfortable with me being the emcee. They wanted someone who was older, and I got the distinct feeling that they were also looking for someone who looked different. Michelle Obama once said, when you feel racism, you know it, you must trust it. There is a feeling that one experiences when the treatment towards you is racist; it hits your soul and sends chills to your bones, and you know that you are being treated a certain way based on the shade of your skin.

I did not back down, which affirmed that they had chosen the right person and that I should be the emcee. The chairwoman also stuck to her decision of choosing me, but I was shocked that for an event honouring women there were women involved who were trying to negate me rather than support me.

I used this experience as fuel for my performance and put my absolute best foot forward, wanting to show them what a young Indian girl can do. The event went so well that at the end of the night a group of men approached me and shared that they were inspired by the things I had said about female empowerment. I will never forget that moment of being vindicated, of having stuck to my guns and having succeeded at doing so.

What did I learn from this incident?

Well, it taught me that in the game of life there will be people who will do their best to disempower those whom they have preconceived notions about. Ironically, these people don't realize that by their very actions they are moving us, as change-makers, closer to our goals because our motivation only gets stronger.

I also learned that courage and confidence are essential tools in instances such as this, and that when we go forward and listen to the voice inside of us that whispers, "You've got this; you are worthy of taking on this role," we negate the white noise of criticism and negativity that tries to bring us down.

The important takeaway in any situation like this is to take on the role of the change-maker, one who effectively and authentically impacts the outcome with positivity and light, and to send light and knowledge to those in need.

I would also like to add that the tools that I use to seed and harvest my spiritual assets of courage, conviction and confidence are all included within the pages of this book. I have found these assets enduring because, whether you realize it or not, every one of us has a singular, unique purpose on this Earth and along every step of the way, the Universe positions us in places and in situations that are right and good for us at that particular juncture in our lives.

And so, it is important to have faith in the Universe, in the belief that the Universe's divine messages fully and aptly acknowledge and respect the abilities that we need to foster in order to deal with the situations that present themselves. We need to have an unwavering faith and confidence in God, or our Higher Power, that we have been specifically chosen and our path created in a way that actualizes our soul purpose.

In fact, the Universe is constantly guiding us and allowing us to experience the kinds of challenges that will make us spiritually and emotionally stronger; there are lessons learned within every struggle. And so, rather than focus on what happened at any given point, my strategy involves appreciating the lessons I have learned and the experiences that I have garnered from every challenging situation.

Let me ask you a quick question: Have you ever heard an explanation for a rose's purpose on this earth?

"That which God said to the Rose, He said to my heart," as

Rumi wrote, explains the beauty and purpose of a rose. A rose has its own distinctly unique purpose in this life, one that is destined to be fulfilled no matter how early or late it blooms.

When a rose blooms, it does so for no other reason than its ordained purpose, which is to bring its perfumed fragrance and beauty to our lives. A rose is perfect with each moment of its existence. It celebrates its state of being, and everyone benefits from its fragrance. We all must focus on our soul purpose and allow ourselves to blossom like a rose.

I have been constantly told throughout my life that I am "too much" or, in other words, that I essentially don't conform to society's standards. I am told that I am too strong; too loud; too powerful. I have also been told that I laugh too much, that I am intimidating, that I am too masculine or not masculine enough. Random people have said to me "I thought you would be different," more direct, or too direct, too affectionate or not friendly enough.

You can see that most of these statements are both contradictory and counter intuitive, opinions that I neither solicit nor invite people to share with me. Truthfully, the random opinions of others are mere rubber darts to me for a wonderfully fascinating and truthful reason, which is, I have and continue to honour the habits that best serve my purpose in life and I practise, on a daily basis, the affirmative work and rituals that you will find outlined in this book.

I live my life with an attitude of gratitude. I embrace the self-fulfilling habits and disciplines to actualize my most auspicious soul purpose. I believe in myself and have a firm ongoing commitment to actualizing my dreams, which are truly the engines for our soul purpose. On a daily basis, I embrace and bless life's struggles, which in turn help me overcome fear and foster the acceptance to welcome the kinds of changes that will effect positive transformation in my life. Through my daily practice of meditation, I collaborate with the spiritual teachings of the

Divine Feminine as I celebrate my empowered inner Goddesses.

Fear and intimidation are rooted in insecurity; realizing this allows both you and me to be strong enough and self-assured enough to ignore what is non-serving, so that we can allow both light and love to illuminate our paths.

And so, I encourage you to insist on actualizing your most authentic self. Be daring. Be unique. Be great. Be authentic. Be YOU.

I would also like to remind you of two important truths. The first is to always be cognizant of the words you say to yourself. What your heart and your spirit hear is what they will do their best to actualize.

So, tell yourself: I can. I will. I am possible. I achieve. I actualize. Another wonderfully fun and enlightening quip that was famously said by Eleanor Roosevelt, and one that I would encourage you to adopt with good humour and a light heart is "Well-behaved women seldom make history."

Life is meant to be joyful, happy and fun. It is a message that is encapsulated within the Universe's intentions.

And so, I embolden you to do your best and refuse to mould yourself into a shape that belies your most fervent wishes and expectations; instead, create an ever-burgeoning mould that is a singular fit for your own destined soul purpose.

Be the power of example and the light that others seek.

I wish you joy, success and light as you embrace and actualize the tenets in this book that have given me access to the privilege of continuously fulfilling my most auspicious, authentic version of myself.

Bloom where you're planted and leave the rest to the gifts and promises and divine powers that the Universe has in store for each one of us.

CHAPTER 2

CELEBRATING LIFE WITH COURAGE, CONVICTION AND UNCONDITIONAL LOVE

"One is love because one is loved.
No reason is needed for loving."

— Paulo Coelho

What is the one wish, the one aspiration that every member of the human race has in common?

Pure and simple, it is the wish to be loved — with no caveats attached.

In truth, is there any better feeling than being told that we are loved, a sharing of the heart and mind that sparks our very spirit with delight and bursts of blushing excitement? And even more magnificent than knowing that we are loved and in fact, loved unconditionally — no "I love you but" or "I love you if" — is the height of pure affirmation and joy.

In fact, hearing as well as saying those three magic words — I love you — is an authentic and personal testament, an overriding flush of acceptance, belonging and empowerment that generates a genuine confirmation and pronouncement that we are a "part of" something great. It is the kind of statement that fills our souls with self-worth, purpose and importance, and brings meaning to virtually every breath that we take.

Interestingly, the three words — I love you — are spoken more often at airports than almost anywhere else.

Why do you think that is?

Well, when a loved one, be it a family member or friend, goes through the airport security gates, we often tend to feel a sense of melancholy and worry. Will "our person" be OK — will they have a safe journey without any of the upsets that travelling often presents? Will they have a wonderful time? Will their feelings or perspectives change as they experience new people and new surroundings?

These kinds of doubts, however, are not attached to the practising of unconditional love, which is aptly addressed by the 13th-century Persian poet, Rumi, who said "Goodbyes are only for those who love with their eyes. Because for those who love with their heart and soul there is no such thing as separation."

So what does it mean to love someone unconditionally? What does a person have to do, what mindset does a person have to adopt in order to process and practise the act of loving a person unequivocally, with no strings attached?

It simply means to love for the sake of love, without asking for something in return. "There are infinite imaginative possibilities when we allow ourselves the freedom to go beyond our perceived limits," says author Harold W. Becker in his book *Unconditional Love: An Unlimited Way of Being* (White Fire Publishing, 2007). I know that my unconditional love for myself and for others — for life itself! — provides the light that reveals my path forward. When we love ourselves unconditionally, we are giving ourselves permission to dream and to love our dreams and believe in them. Anything our minds can envision we can go on to build.

The very idea of unconditional love is a phenomenon that has enough desire and "want" attached to it that library shelves throughout the world groan under the tomes written on this subject.

If we look at how love is defined by individuals who have reached a state of enlightenment, or are pursuing their soul purpose, their interpretation of this emotion is linked by the common thread of awareness and the possibilities awakened by love itself. In fact, spiritual leaders throughout the ages have waxed poetic about the benefits of unconditional love when it is bestowed upon our family and friends on a daily basis.

American spiritual leader Ram Dass said that love is awareness, a value that can only be awakened through the very practice of love itself.

The potential for unconditional love exists deep inside all of us. Such love doesn't need a reason to be expressed or an object to be focused on. Rather, as the spiritual teacher, yogi, psychologist and writer Ram Dass and others have explained, it is a state of being human, part of our intrinsic and miraculous makeup.

Unfortunately, somewhere along the line, there are those who, in the pursuit of controlling or manipulating a relationship or a situation, make love a transactional thing. Their proffering of love is bracketed in parenthesis and expectations: "If you do this for me, I will love you. If you love me, then I will love you." A true commitment to the act of loving unconditionally should be love for the sake of love, with no conditions or strings attached.

Rumi said: "If words come from the heart, they will enter the heart. If they come from the tongue, they will not pass beyond the ears."

I find poignant inspiration in Rumi's teachings because he lived his life in the pursuit of actualizing his soul purpose. He did not call himself a philosopher or a poet because he felt that philosophy was linked to logical thinking and poetry was limited in its framework. Rumi wanted to speak freely and without constraints about the love that was in his heart, which is exactly what he did. It is this same kind of energy and confidence that I hope to awaken in you within the pages of this book.

And so, what does unconditional love mean to me?

Well, first of all, in order for love to be genuinely proffered, it needs to be unconditional, which first and foremost means that there is no heart space for negotiations. This is a tenet that applies both to us and to others. I don't believe in saying, "I love you, but ..." because, when we use that three-letter denigrating word "but" we are essentially negating the love we tender because of the conditions we have attached to that love. Instead, I replace the conditions inherent in the word "but" with the conjunction "and," because love should always be used within a positive context. Love is an energy force that should, I believe, power our relationships with our family and friends on a daily basis. When we say, "I will only love you if you do this," or "if you take me here" or "do this for me," we are not engaging in pure acts of unconditional love, rather we make it transactional. When we love unconditionally we are genuinely, and with an open heart, committing to offering our love freely without some kind of expected repayment attached. Otherwise, we are offering love with "strings attached" — in effect, conditional love. This is a situation that creates inequality in relationships, as well as power and control imbalances. And what is just as important is that, as individuals, we need to realize that we have to treat ourselves in the same way, with the same respect and kindness, without any conditions we might place on unconditional self-love. It is counterproductive to look in the mirror and say, "I will love myself once I lose twenty pounds." Or "I will give myself props when I get this promotion," or "I land this partner that I am attracted to." No. We have to love ourselves in our heart, in the mirror every morning and every night, unequivocally and unconditionally.

When we genuinely love ourselves, it becomes a part of our strength, a part of our aura. Others notice it because it illuminates and manifests itself in our daily interactions with others. Our connections with ourselves set the tone for our relationships with others.

As a part of that, our words and our tone, the things we say to others, define our relationships. Our words are magic; when they are loving, kind and empathetic they have the ability to change people's outlooks and how they move throughout their day.

Our words can make a child giggle, a partner laugh or a stranger smile.

Also, what we tell ourselves becomes a self-fulfilling prophecy. Our words hold the power to unite, to comfort and to heal. When we promise a friend or colleague that we will do this or do that right away, more often than not, we act on our promises.

But when we make promises to ourselves, how many times do we keep them? We promise ourselves that we will engage in better self-care; we will go to the gym more often; drink less; eat better; meditate daily; listen better; and be more mindfully present. But how often do we keep these promises of unconditionally loving ourselves instead of putting our work or the needs of others before our own?

Our own words, especially with ourselves, are like magic — they cast spells of loving intention and respect. Words have the power to create and inspire, so I encourage you to listen to these messages from the heart.

In his book *Unconditional Love is ... Appreciating Aspects of Life* (White Fire Publishing, 2010), Harold W. Becker identifies peace, harmony, compassion, creativity and abundance as qualities that come from the essence of who we are and embody "the heart of unconditional love," and advises us to tap into our positive energies, using our courage and gratitude to enrich our personal understanding and experience of love.

I have learned to love myself unconditionally by adhering to the above principles and these following philosophies:

I speak words to myself and to others that come from a loving place in my heart.

I choose my words with love.

I focus on loving actions and friendships that lift me up.
I surround myself with the people who I know are true-hearted in their desire to see me succeed in actualizing my soul purpose.
I surround myself with love, encouragement and faith.
I refuse to speak words that do not serve the true source of my unconditional love and unconditional forgiveness.
I use my energy to seek out my truth.
I commit to allowing life to be beautiful and seeing grace and blessings everywhere I go.

It is also important to remember that the way that we treat others is how we need to treat ourselves — with love, kindness, empathy and respect. This is not a selfish concept, but rather an act of self-love. There isn't a person alive who does not, at many crossroads along life's path, experience the hardships, travails and struggles inherent in living life on life's terms. But when we do the work of believing in ourselves, acting with the conviction of our beliefs and treating ourselves and others with the kind of unconditional love that carries no judgment, we are equipped with the ability to stop the negative, recriminating tapes before we even hit play.

What we can be grateful for, instead, are the lessons that the hard days in life teach us, and we can be thankful to the Universe for giving us the courage and strength to withstand the situations or painful circumstances we are going through.

A loving spirit liberates us; it is a force like no other. It is invisible — something that we cannot see or physically grasp; and while it can't be measured, it is powerful enough to transform us within the moment and offer more joy than any material possession could possibly ever offer. When we emanate love, it is omnipresent; we do not have to search for it because it becomes a fundamental part of our heart source.

Jesuit paleontologist Pierre Teilhard de Chardin said "We're not human beings having a spiritual experience. We are spiritual beings having a human experience."

An easy-to-grasp example of unconditional self-love is illustrated by the steps we are instructed to take by flight attendants when our aircraft is about to take flight. It is a concept that took me a while to grasp because at first I considered it to be a selfish action. Anyone who has ever been on a plane has watched the flight attendants instruct the passengers on what they should do if the aircraft loses air pressure. We are told that when the oxygen masks drop down from their chambers, we are to put the mask on ourselves before helping anyone else.

The first few times that I heard this I was confused, because my first inclination is to always help someone who is vulnerable or compromised — a mother with her infant child or an elderly person who is having trouble breathing. However, I came to realize that if I didn't put on my own mask, so that I would have access to the air flow I need to maintain my own strength and fortitude, I would be too weak or incapacitated to help the people who needed my assistance the most.

A friend of mine, "Tarot Lori," whom I like to call my Goddess sister, often reads my tarot cards as a means to guiding me along life's powerful path. Funnily, the card that Lori frequently pulls for me is the "Four of Wands." The reason that this card is so serendipitous for me can be found in its meaning, which is that "Self-care needs to be prioritized, not just because it fills your tank and makes you better for everyone and everything else, but because you deserve it. You deserve to prioritize your time and energy because nobody else will. If the plane is going down, you're supposed to put on your own mask before worrying about anyone else and not compromise your own safety."

Or, as Paulo Coelho says, "When you are loved, there's no need at all to understand what's happening, because everything happens within you." When we are loved, we can do anything in creation.

When my heart is full of love, it has the courage to be free, to openly surrender to the practice of fulfilling my soul purpose.

An affirmation that I say, and one I encourage you to also embrace, is this light-filled proclamation that will allow you to sprinkle your day with unconditional love-speak.

I am full of courage.
I am surrounded by white light.
My energy is positive and attracts like-minded positive energy.
I am full of confidence.
My love for myself is deep, pure and creates a light within.

I would like to pause here for a moment and ask you a question before we delve further into what I like to call the language of the heart.

Do you often — or ever — take a moment to check in with your heart — to say the kinds of affirmations that will make it beat stronger and more lovingly — for you?

How would you rate your ability to talk to your heart; to practise unconditional love for yourself and for others? When you take time to speak directly to your heart, it creates a spiritual state of being that amplifies your ability to love yourself unconditionally.

I physically speak to my heart every day. I ask my heart how is feeling, what it is feeling, and my heart always speaks back. Sometimes my heart reveals things to me that I did not know I was feeling. It helps me move past and through those feelings and emotions. When you speak to your heart, it further allows you to speak more love to yourself and to others.

An important factor when proffering unconditional love to others, for the sake of our own self-respect and our own self-love, is to ensure that the people to whom we are offering our love are worthy of our vulnerability, loyalty and commitment. The term "unconditional love" does not mean love without limits or bounds. It means "I offer you my love freely without condition or without expectation of repayment." My personal mandate is to love fully and unconditionally, but also to share and reciprocate it with those who love me proudly and fiercely.

Boundaries are essential components of friendship, according to Iyanla Vanzant, the American life coach, inspirational speaker and former host of OWN's *Iyanla: Fix My Life*, who thinks you need them even as a condition for being a true friend to yourself. As you learn how to trust and become loving to yourself, your boundaries are the guard rails that provide for your safety. When you trust yourself and the people you share your life with, you can permit your boundaries to be porous when you choose to let people in. And like physical guard rails, they don't need to be tested — just knowing that they're there can gift us with a sense of security even as we move forward and acknowledge our own responsibility in creating our past experiences, our present and our future.

Interestingly, in relationships where the love may not be what our soul needs, where the loving by one is not equally shared, not equally matched nor respected with integrity by the other partner, situations arise where boundary lines are crossed. Sometimes, we choose to shift that boundary, and again and again, in order to meet the other person's needs. At this point, the person who is loving unconditionally and with a pure heart is no longer in a relationship that is built on self-love because they have compromised themselves. I offer unconditional love to others knowing that I also will not compromise my self-respect nor integrity in these relationships.

As you read this, pause a moment and have an honest conversation with your heart. Listen to the whisper of your heart's language around how you perceive yourself in the relationships you are in, and be sure that the very essence of your being and the fundamentals that drive your soul purpose are being lovingly honoured within your relationships. When we speak from the heart, the other people in our lives will, through osmosis, receive it within their hearts.

Do you speak the language of love — and, if so, how do you translate it in your daily life?

For me, speaking the language of love encompasses the daily act of checking in with my heart several times a day. I do that by asking my heart "OK, heart, how are we feeling about what's going on in my life today?"

I usually follow up with the questions that are on my mind — ones that I am hoping my heart will whisper the answer or offer a solution to — by saying affirmations such as this one:

I am open to listening to you, my heart, and I am willing to embrace the wisdom that best suits my situation.
I am open and willing to follow the path that you show me.
I know unequivocally that the language of the heart is always going to be pure, and it is always going to be true.
It is a voice that never leads me astray or down the wrong path.

In Coelho's *The Alchemist,* the main character, who is referred to as "the boy," says that his heart often alarmed him when there was danger present. In other words, when we are in tune with our hearts, it will always send us a warning — a fluttering or fast-paced signal — when something that is about to happen is encompassed in negativity or non-serving results. The more we listen to our heart, the more we will be attuned to its warnings.

Our first priority should be to understand and master the love that we have for ourselves in order to ensure that we love ourselves unconditionally.

"Don't give into your fears. If you do, you won't be able to talk to your heart," Coelho writes in *The Alchemist.*

We search for purpose, not understanding that our life's purpose was given to us the second we came into this world.

To love, and to love unconditionally, is our true purpose in life. Whether we show love with kindness and in service to others or simply with happiness, we are speaking the language of love.

It is so important to live life with happiness! But what does to live life *with* happiness, not *for* happiness mean exactly? In our busy harried lives, we often tend to live our lives in a conditional, full-of-parameters kind of way. We say, "I will be happy when I go on that vacation, when I receive that promotion, when I am able to purchase that home." But when we place our happiness on the "when," we ignore the happiness and confidence of living in the "now." We focus so much on "being happy when" that as we go through our daily routines, we set ourselves up, in fact, self-sabotage ourselves, to remain disenchanted until we reach the goals we have set for ourselves. But this is false. True happiness lies within every moment that we are here. We are blessed to take each breath, blessed to see the sun set and the moon rise. We are blessed, and when we place our happiness in the future we forget just how blessed we truly are, each minute of every day.

"God gave us the gift of life; it is up to us to give ourselves the gift of living well," as famously stated by Voltaire, the French enlightenment philosopher. Within this sage wisdom is the encapsulation of the Divine principle of living and loving with unconditional love. I love to make people smile and even laugh, and I go through life always wanting to be a part of someone's happiness, even if for a moment. I make time in my day to send out love messages to my loved ones, or even just an "I miss you" so they feel loved. One of my secrets if I am feeling down or having "one of those days" is to always tell myself, in order to pick myself up, that I am going to send out love to those around me because I have the confidence to know that when I send out that love, my heart will then be full of happiness. And it always brightens my soul and day!

What better way can any one of us serve each other with love than to be the reason, the epicentre of inspiring happiness within those we touch, while at the same time being an empathetic partner in their grief?

We are "here to be here for each other," no matter what life presents; an ultimate gift to be mindfully present in the moment, for the moment, for each other.

And no matter how many opportunities have been lost, there is always more goodness that is ready to be created, more opportunities to be explored and fulfilled. No matter what you have done with what has been, you now have the possibilities for what can be. And what can be is yours to build, to fashion, in the best way you can imagine. The goodness of what can be is far more powerful than any memory of what has been, so let yourself embrace it fully. What can be begins in this moment, what can be comes from your thoughts, your actions, the discipline, passion and commitment with which you live from this point forward.

So just how do we do that?

First of all, we need to look in the mirror and embrace the courage to honestly and humbly identify all of the traits that we love about ourselves. It is critical that we embrace them with love and respect. Then we need to list the aspects we would like to work on and embrace those traits as well. Do not dishonour yourself by looking in the mirror and picking yourself apart, thinking or saying unkind words to the image that is innocently looking back at you. Embrace all of the quirks, positive traits and talents that you have because these are what makes you YOU, and declare to yourself that you are full of confidence, courage, conviction and love.

If I were to ask you to think of someone you admire and then tell me the reasons why, you could probably spend a good five to ten minutes listing the things you love about that person. However, if I then turned that spotlight on you, you would not be nearly as kind nor complimentary to yourself. You may get to three traits about yourself but after that, it would be difficult. But I'll let you in on a little secret, one that will uplift you and buoy your confidence. Each one of us has the ability to shine pure and bright; we just need to know how to light the match to spark the flame. Within this light, I promise you that you will recognize your courage within, which will, in turn, build confidence in your abilities and allow you to move forward with absolute conviction and self-confidence.

As my sister Shelley says, my confidence has inspired her with the courage to acknowledge her gut feeling and her intuition as she goes about her day.

Once the deep well of our soul is filled with happiness from within, we will attract positive light and energy, for love is not encapsulated in just one thing or one person. Unconditional love shines through in everything the sun touches, every living being that has been created by God.

Love is the energy that binds us all together. It is the energy that allows us to achieve our soul purpose. It gives us the energy to actualize our dreams on the path to becoming our most authentic selves. In truth, when we allow our lives to be lived with unconditional love, we manifest our most authentic self.

My parents have a 100-year-old cherry tree in their backyard that blossoms every spring. During the quiet and isolating days of 2020, when the global COVID-19 pandemic was at its peak, I found myself drawn to the elegance of this tree, to its beauty as it grew toward the sunlight. Its tiny buds, having withstood the harsh winter, were bursting forth in breathtaking pink fragrant blossoms as they reached heavenward to fulfil their soul purpose of bringing great magic and beauty to those who were mindfully present and wholly appreciative.

This tree is symbolic for me, a statement on how I should be living my life — with purpose and intent, free of the daily distractions and white noise of everyday life. I became acutely aware that the cherry blossoms did not care about the other trees in the yard, neither bending nor bowing to see whether there were other flowers that were more colourful or beautiful. They did not compare themselves to other fragrant blossoms and decide that they were not good enough or worthy enough to be showcasing their very presence. Instead, they were actualizing the purpose that the Universe had given them, which was to celebrate the new season of spring, new life after a long winter and the return of warm sensual breezes that hailed the advent of spring.

This cherry tree reminded me, also, that pure love enters into our heart when we surrender to the mysterious touch of the divine, for love is the power that moves creation, the force that inspires destiny, the power that ignites manifestation.

Rumi, who said "The power of love came into me, and I became fierce like a lion, then tender like the evening star," spoke often about the power of love, that the lion strength he garnered from it allowed him to feel that nothing in his life was a challenge, he felt that powerful. He also admired the magical purpose of the stars in the evening sky, and how they bring light to the darkest of nights, a true comparison to the power that is love.

Two additional and highly important components that are key to loving ourselves as well as others unconditionally are ones we are all well familiar with.

The first factor that stands in the way of our loving unconditionally is a human foible that is common to many, if not all of us — the familiar and ubiquitous habit of judging others.

There is an old adage that tells us that when we point a finger at someone in judgment, we have four fingers pointing back at us. So, if instead of judging ourselves, which then becomes a mirror for criticizing and judging others, we were to fill ourselves with the spiritual flow of love, tolerance, courage, conviction and confidence, how much better would our lives be? How about the lives of those who we touch on a continual basis?

By letting go of our pasts and realizing that there is nothing we can do to change them and then joining that to a willingness to forgive ourselves with a loving, compassionate heart, we will come to a place of childlike wonder, enlightenment and grace.

This state of well-being will allow us to love who we were, who we are now and the distance in between that we have lovingly traversed.

I have found that as I have been able to successfully attain the mindset of loving myself unconditionally, I have enough self-confidence and enough self-love to take criticisms with a light heart and with a sense of detachment, most especially when they are unfounded.

In Don Miguel Ruiz's book, *The Four Agreements, A Practical Guide to Personal Freedom* (Amber-Allen Publishing, 1997), which you will read more about in Chapter 4: "Embracing Habit and Discipline to Actualize Your Most Auspicious Soul Purpose," you will discover that Ruiz's "First Agreement," which advises us to not take things personally, is advice that you will find helpful and one that deeply resonates with me.

More often than not, when someone lashes out, when someone says or does hurtful things to us, it does not necessarily have anything to do with us personally but, rather, could quite possibly be due to a hurt that is deep inside the other person.

We are all vested with the personal power to not take things personally. If we don't get an answer back from a text we have sent, or a reply to a phone message that we have left, we should respect that the other person is most likely as busy as we are. Maybe they are waiting to respond to us at a time that allows them to send back a more intentional and thoughtful message. Maybe the person wants to send a message that reflects their love or their friendship and are too tied up at that particular moment to get back to us. I cannot stress enough the importance of not letting our egos get in the way, which in turn often causes misunderstandings and misplaced resentments.

Rather than getting in a huff, I celebrate the people that are available to me at any particular moment and revel in my sense of humour and my love of laughter. I respect that other people are busy, too, and that maybe they are not responding to me because they want to reply with a message that comes from their heart.

One of my favourite quotes that my mother, Rashmi, often says to me is one that has kept me consistently on the path of humility, forgiveness and empathy. It is one that my heart constantly prompts me to remember when I am in situations that speak loudly to her advice: "Don't lose your loved ones because of your ego. Instead lose your ego in front of your loved ones.

And that is exactly what loving unconditionally is, the ability to push our ego out of the way and show our personal vulnerabilities. It is having the humility to say "I love you unconditionally." It is having the sensitivity to say "I need you and I think about you." The second key that I've found has helped me to unlock the possibilities inherent in unconditional love is the grace of forgiveness. Forgiveness is like love. It only works if it is unconditionally embraced. It is a truism that it is only when we genuinely and honestly forgive a person or a situation that we will be able to walk our path forward. Forgiveness is an integral part of self-love.

In fact, Dr. Martin Luther King Jr. famously said "I have decided to stick with love. Hate is too great a burden to bear."

So, what does forgiveness look like to me?

Well, I can honestly say that if I am involved in a disagreement or a fight, it is not in my nature to stay mad. The second that the other person apologizes with a genuine and pure heart, my forgiveness is immediate. When we don't take things personally, we are able to forge ahead and forgive easily. The thing about forgiveness is that if we don't forgive unconditionally, we end up carrying resentments around in our heart.

And paradoxically, when we don't forgive the person who we feel has wronged us, it doesn't hurt them — it hurts us. We acquire a resentment that becomes a breeding ground for anger, upset, irritability and despondency — resentments that can affect us physically and emotionally. Our energy and perspective toward that person becomes so affected that, even when we meet someone who just reminds us of that person, our stomachs start to churn. It is a mindset that we must divest ourselves of because in truth we are really the only person shouldering this real or perceived hurt.

Thích Nhất Hạnh teaches us that when someone hurts us we need to go to the person to alleviate our resentment, a negative emotion that can easily overshadow any light that is trying to shine through. Because sometimes our hurts come from our own misperceptions of a situation, Thích Nhất Hạnh advises to carefully examine our own hearts before blaming our suffering on others. If we do determine that someone else's actions are hurting us, though, we should gently but confidently ask them, without confrontation, why they have done or said something that has hurt us. By doing so we are opening a portal in our heart to them that will lessen our suffering.

There are times however, and this is admittedly one of the hardest things to do, when and if we don't get an apology, we just have to walk away and continue on our journey of practising the art of complete and unconditional forgiveness.

But how do we effectively do that — how do we let go of the feeling of being wronged and shrug off the shackles of resentment? Well, what I do is have an honest conversation with the Universe. I ask for help — unconditionally — and the ability to help me see the person or the situation with a new lens, a new perspective.

Once again, it is important that we leave the outcome to the Universe. We need to let go and let be and not allow our egos to get in the way.

A man once asked Buddha: "How can I achieve the happiness I seek?"

Buddha told him: "Remove I, that's ego. Remove want, that's desire. Then, all you are left with is happiness."

As the author of our own stories, we are fully equipped and accountable for controlling our own destinies and our own ability to love unconditionally and to do so without judgment or prejudice.

I recommend using this affirmation to practise the above principles:

Love with no excuses.
Live with no regret.
Love unconditionally.
Forgive openly.
Laugh freely.

I am a big believer in connecting with the Universe as a way to allow any negativity I might encounter to be alleviated. My Higher Power then gifts me with the open-minded willingness to embrace all that I meet with unconditional love, confidence and conviction.

Lastly, when we love unconditionally, we show up for the people we love. One of the biggest gifts we can bestow on someone we love is to be there for that person when we know they are in pain and are suffering. And as a part of that, when we show up, we need to commit to being mindfully present. This means that we give the person our undivided attention, no cell phones, no tablets, no laptops — and to have no agenda of our own.

When I practise unconditional love for a friend who is going through hard times, I ensure that I am mindfully present, and that rather than looking for solutions to their problems, and thus detaching from what they are saying so I can think of a response, I just sit there and listen — truly listen. I find that if my mind is in chatter mode, it is so busy recording the moment that I am not fully present. There is an art to "being in the moment," but unfortunately in many cases, mindfully listening has become a lost art. Oftentimes, a lot of words are spoken, a lot of defensive positions taken — one person is right, the other person is wrong — but when we learn to listen with an open heart and a closed ego, major changes can be effected as the language of the heart is spoken.

When we listen, truly listen, with not just our physical presence, but emotionally and mentally as well — we are practising unconditional love. We love and care about the person enough to put our own interests aside as we mindfully listen. It is important that we don't engage in an agenda, waiting for our turn to provide a solution, defend or justify our own or someone else's behaviour and actions. Listening is a two-way street, not a dead-end alley. And when we are truly present, we are gifting our person with the best present we could ever give them — our full, unbridled attention and love.

Everything we need to achieve our soul purpose, to love unconditionally and to forgive purely, can be found within us.

So how do we find the key to unlock this way of living?

For me, the key to my happiness has been, and continues to be, a willingness to being open to the Universe's guidance and promptings. I adhere to the philosophy that when the student is ready, the teacher appears. As such, I make sure that I am always open to opportunities that present themselves because I know that my willingness unlocks life's abundance.

I top up my faith in the Universe and in myself on a daily basis because I know that with faith my fears have no chance to survive. They have no fodder on which to feed. In order to negate any fears that might try to present themselves, I know that I need to keep my faith topped up, a practice that you will hear me summarize several times throughout this book. When I use my faith-based investment as my foundation, it allows me to fashion the bricks I use to build my soul purpose's mansion.

In fact, the best advice that I can give you as you embrace unconditional love is to intrinsically change how you think about fear. Rather than ride the coattails of the well-worn and highly negative acronym FEAR — "Fear everything and run" — instead, look in the mirror and tell yourself: "Face everything and rise." I guarantee it will create a seismic mind shift and a new positive attitude on how to face your most tumultuous and scary challenges.

And with this newfound faith, I promise you that even the darkest corners of your heart will be filled with the light of hope and possibilities. For when we have faith, anything and everything is possible, even that which first seems impossible.

Any time you feel like giving up, feeling that what you seek is impossible or will take too much effort or time, I want you to repeat the following affirmation to yourself:

> **Impossible is a word that is full of possibilities, Because in the very parsing of the word, what at first seemed inconceivable is now probable.**
> **I AM POSSIBLE.**
> **When we believe in ourselves, the possible is always an option.**
> **When I am in the midst of tumult and chaos, I remind myself that God and the Universe have my back; they know that I have the strength to get through the situations in front of me.**
> **My inner happiness is based on my confidence in myself, which in turn allows me to move forward with courage and conviction.**

As I mentioned earlier in this chapter, courage is not always wrapped in thunder, lightning or a roaring voice, but oftentimes presents itself as the soft voice at the end of the day encouraging us to try again tomorrow.

As children, we were fully open to both giving and receiving love. Our hearts were full of unfettered innocence and the joy of wonderment and new experiences. We had faith in our parents and caretakers; we had a blind faith that everything was OK, and so we smiled openly and laughed often as we explored new opportunities with our curiosity and inexhaustible energy. We had a playful aura because we had faith in everyone around us.

We intuitively trusted that our soul purpose as children was to be happy, trusting and playfully focused. We intuitively knew that there was a force greater than ourselves taking care of us.

How different our lives would be if we had been able to sustain that childlike innocence as adults, with that brilliant trust in our fellow beings. And how wonderful it would be to once again find that playfulness as adults, remembering and understanding that there is still a force greater than us taking care of our spiritual needs. Whether that is a belief in the purpose of the Universe, in the forces of nature, or in the direction of our lives, if we were able to put our faith and trust once again in the powers that be, as we once did as children, we could surrender our fears and worries to this Higher Power, knowing that we are each on this planet to fulfil our own unique soul purposes.

If we could once again connect with our childlike sense of innocence and trust, we would intuitively know that it is our divine right to express ourselves and not try to camouflage or filter our intentions. When we live our lives with confidence and conviction, we are well and truly capable of allowing our hearts to live with love, magic and a wonderful sense of unabated curiosity.

I have also found that being curious brings an energy to my life that makes me feel light-hearted, youthful and mysterious. When I am curious, magic and mystery follow in my wake, which in turn brings me closer to manifesting my soul purpose. It is a path that is embedded in the concept of loving myself consistently and unconditionally.

Love is the purpose of life. Faith is its elixir.
Love is the power that moves creation.
Love is the force that inspires destiny.
Love is the most important power that exists.

Nothing is impossible for pure love.
Stay close to those who are pure of heart,
Because love attracts love.

Rumi says, "The inspiration you seek is already within you. Be silent and listen."

When we quiet our mind, we allow the Universe to speak to us. When we hear the white noise of fear and worry, we can trust the Universe to guide us and surround us with the light that will show us the path we are seeking. When we allow our minds to sit in silence, our heart will have the chance to let go of its fear and sadness, and instead will replenish itself with joy and happiness.

We can master the ability to quiet our minds through meditation, which you will learn more about in Chapter 8 – "Meditation: Collaborating with the Spiritual Teachings of the Divine Feminine."

I have found that my meditation practice has gifted me with the power to heal my mind, body, soul and spirit. It has empowered me with a deep spiritual connection to the Universe and the power to actualize my dreams. It has allowed me to feel the ethereal power of divine love and, ultimately, as I am sure you know by now, is my soul's purpose in life — for the best way, the most divine way to connect to our spiritual intentions is through the practice of unconditional love.

Another key life value that is integral to how I manifest my divinely directed intentions is wrapped in my daily practice of welcoming each and every day with a courageous heart and a tiger spirit.

Courage, whose original root definition comes from the Latin word *cor*, or "heart," originally meant the speaking of one's mind or "telling one's heart." The definition has since evolved to encompass the mental or moral strength to "venture, persevere and withstand danger, fear or difficulty."

However, courage does not need to present itself as a flashy blast of audacity or daring. Rather it is the quiet acts of lifting ourselves — or others — up on difficult, challenging or painful days. And courage is not limited to superhuman efforts of physicality. Courage is also deeply embedded in our everyday moral, intellectual, disciplined and empathetic actions. It is the act of taking that step forward and being accountable as others take a step back, who might be commiserating about the tragedy or unfairness of a situation, but not actually plucking up their courage and saying "This is not right — how can I help and be of service?"

When we wear the mantle of courage, our daily approach and attitude toward situations allow us to do our best to the best of our abilities. When we drown our attempts to be our most authentic and auspicious selves by self-recriminations of, "We should have done this" or "should have done that" or "we could have done or said this," we are not honouring our courageous intentions to honour the talents and the abilities that we have been gifted with by the Universe. It is at those times when we persevere, when we don't give in and we don't give up that our Higher Power acknowledges our efforts and comes to our aid.

It is also the understanding that, if we didn't make any progress today, find the applicable solution or achieve what we needed to do — for whatever reason and through no fault of our own — we will get out of bed, get out of our slump and try again tomorrow.

As American writer and humourist Mark Twain said, "Courage is resistance to fear, mastery of fear, not absence of fear."

Courage is also about the willingness to open our eyes and embrace rather than run from situations that are challenging. I have found that when I am willing I always find a way to resolve the issues in front of me because I have the courage to do so and the faith to know that all is well, even if it does not feel like that in the present moment. And being willing to make a difference affords me with the possibilities I may not have discerned if my mind was otherwise engaged or if I was not present in the moment.

As a positive way to recognize and replenish my daily reserves of courage, I sit in quiet meditation and whisper the following affirmation to my spirit narrative:

When I work hard, I have found that God is always there to buoy me up at the very moment I need that extra hand of courage and encouragement.
The Universe also smiles on my determination and bravery and inspires me with the belief that anything and everything is possible; that even the impossible is possible with faith in both me and the Universe.
I am.
I can.
I will.

Change is life's responsibility and transformation is ours. Each and every one of us is capable of changing the world — if only in our own backyard, our own corner of the neighbourhood — by the simple and accessible acts of living with courage, conviction and unconditional love.

I believe that love is an energy that exists within each one of us as we live life with a heart that is glowing with positive, beautiful, radiant energy. I also firmly believe that, when our souls are enlightened, we are able to bring about and nurture the possible out of the impossible.

Every language in the world understands the communal light-filled emotion that is love. Our hearts are made from love, with love, in love. Our hearts are intuitive and have ways to whisper secrets to us that only we are personally able to understand on the most intimate level. Our hearts have built-in GPSes "God-Propelled Signs," that guide us toward the light that is unconditional love if we are open and willing to receive it.

Take a look at the people around you. Are they people who

elevate you, who lift you up in times of need? Do they love you unconditionally and support you in the same way?

As Ram Dass said, "We are all just walking each other home," meaning that we are all walking this journey called life together; one that, when we do our best to live it in a spirit of courage, conviction and unconditional love, will allow us to connect with the Universe or our Higher Power of choice, with joy, positivity and kindness. The meaning of life is realized by exquisitely actualizing our own personal soul purposes.

"'Tell me the truth,' I asked love. 'What are you?' 'I am the everlasting life,' love said," as Rumi famously wrote. When we follow our heart, we will always and unequivocally be led by love to love.

As theoretical physicist Albert Einstein said, "There are only two ways to live your life. One is as though nothing is a miracle. The other is as though everything is a miracle."

CHAPTER 3

THE DIVINE GIFTS OF LIVING LIFE WITH AN ATTITUDE OF GRATITUDE

"An attitude of gratitude creates blessings. Help yourself by helping others. You have the most powerful weapons on Earth — love and prayer."

— Mother Teresa

I approach this chapter on gratitude with — well, with gratitude — excitement and a thankful heart. In fact, my joy for gratitude is such that I consider it a true privilege to share my thoughts, feelings and commitment with you as you take journey with me through this book. It is what drives everything I do, from the smallest of things — whether it is greeting the sun as it comes up over the horizon or sending messages of love to my friends early in the morning so they can start their day with unexpected positivity.

So, just what is gratitude, and what practices does gratitude embody?

To me, gratitude is my connection to both my inner spirit and my purpose in the Universe.

Gratitude can turn a smile into laughter, a problem into a blessing, a missed opportunity into a leap of faith and possibility.

AUSPICIOUS

The more gratitude we have, the more we are able to connect to our soul purpose and inner spirit.

It is simple appreciation for all of the little gifts that the Universe bestows on us on a continuous and daily basis. When we practise gratitude, even towards ourselves, we are showing respect, grace, faith, forgiveness and empathy to ourselves and to those around us who also benefit from our grateful heart. A quiet, gentle word of encouragement or affection, both given and received, and the practice of giving thanks renew both my soul and my intentions. In truth, it is the gearshift that alters and drives my perspective on a daily basis. Having gratitude actualizes the three Cs in my life, courage, conviction and confidence, for when I say small prayers of gratitude my very spirit is lifted and empowered.

Interestingly, many of us only think of being grateful when we are dealing with, or in the midst of, dire circumstances. We send supplications heavenward, telling the Universe: "If you fix this problem, or if you get me out of this relationship safely and whole, I will be forever grateful."

We all have difficult days and come up against many struggles while living life on life's terms, and it is during these times that I reflect on what I need to be grateful for — the simple gifts of people, circumstances or opportunities in my life that represent the grace that is gratitude. It brings much light into my life.

In fact, during the day, if I am faced with a problem or a challenge, I do my best to look at the situation as a valuable lesson that I need to learn. I do my best to understand what it is I need to garner from the particular challenge and how I can go about handling it with grace and gratitude. In order to do so, I meditate, pray and ask the Universe to lovingly listen to my question and provide me with any sort of guidance. What is important and what we all have to realize, however, is that the solution we pray for may not be the Universe's whispered answer in our ear. Rather, what often happens is that the Universe listens, hears us and then proceeds to answer our prayers by providing us with a different perspective and — this is key — it might be one that we may not be interested in embracing. But we have to be open to this new way of thinking, of considering that what the Universe is telling us, that this is the best possible outcome, rather than pushing back because it is not what we really want to do or it doesn't meet with our stubborn will. Staying stuck in a negative mindset, surrounded by unhelpful statements such as "Everything is horrible; I can never catch a break; why do things never work out for me?" is not only the complete opposite of being grateful, it also does not help problem-solve nor light the way to a beneficial solution. Instead, if we say, "God, thank you for this problem in front of me. Please help me to see this situation with a different perspective knowing that I am grateful for any guidance you can give me," I can assure you that a solution will appear.

We have all experienced situations in our lives when we sincerely wanted to be a part of new adventures or new relationships or new friendships but somehow, as time went on, our wishes were not granted. In these situations, we have to tell ourselves that the very people, places or things we desired so passionately were not granted to us for a reason. This reason, over time, the Universe will reveal to us. It is then that we should thank God, in fact, thank the Universe, for looking after our best interests, when we could not see the path. I have found that the best way to manifest my desired intention is to say, "Universe, if you see this wish of mine as being a positive step forward, a positive influence in my life, please hear my prayer and provide me with the solution that is the best for my soul purpose."

Surrendering the outcome of our prayers to the Universe and being open to the answer we receive gifts us with a new or different perspective. And as many of us have learned, when the Universe gifts us with an alternate answer, it is blessing us and protecting us from what could have been one of the worst possible scenarios for us in hindsight. Ultimately, the Universe frequently saves us from ourselves, which with good humour and thankful spirit, we need to be grateful for.

Funnily, that is gratitude at its most magnificent.

As such, learn to be grateful for yourself — for who you are, for the very traits that make you unique to actualizing your soul purpose and intent in life. Celebrate the fact that you are you — and no one else can do you better.

The act of practising gratitude looks different for everyone and is unique to each person. For me, because I have been practising gratitude for such a long time, the very act of doing so has become an innate part of me. When things happen around me that are challenging, tough or overwhelming, I immediately look at all I have to be grateful for.

In early 2023, when Turkey was hit with devastating earthquakes, I thanked God that I was born in Canada. I also thanked God that I had the financial resources and manpower to help the citizens of Turkey. And help is what I did, working with a team to ensure that the Gupta Family Foundation could successfully deliver goods to areas in and around Turkey that did not have easy access to the essentials of life and needed assistance.

In my meditation practice, I show my gratitude by gratefully acknowledging that I have this time to give myself as I mindfully set my intentions for the day. I gratefully greet each new day with light, and with clear intentions around what I want to achieve in the next eight to ten hours. I give thanks for my job, my friends and my health — simple things that we all tend to take for granted but are important and life-changing gifts in our lives. Practising acts of daily gratitude has become an ongoing and consistent habit for me — a discipline, really, because I know that the energy I attract throughout my day is based on how genuinely sincere I am about welcoming the day's blessings into my heart.

As such, I give thanks for the day that is ahead of me — I am grateful for my colleagues and for the work that we do together.

I am also grateful for the different opinions that people present, and rather than push back on their ideas because they may not fit into my plan, I leave room in my agenda to listen with an open heart to the solutions they present. The purpose of life is to keep evolving — to attain and invite into our lives the Universe's messages of love, hope and joy, all of which are key to helping us actualize our soul purposes.

When I go hard in the gym and I am at the end of my session, I always sit on my mat and take a moment to thank my body for being healthy enough to work out.

One of my most favourite things to do — and, quite honestly, what my soul purpose demands — is to spread love and kindness, for when we feel love and kindness from someone else, we immediately feel the warm nurturing glow of gratitude. More often than not, this spiritual top-up then inspires us to bestow love and kindness on others.

I turn my gratitude into kindness for others because everyone deserves love. I want others to feel loved and blessed. For example, I randomly send love texts to my friends, especially when I know they need a quick pick-me-up. Saying "I love you" is powerful, kind and meaningful. When I feel that others need love, I freely give it, hoping that my love and genuine affection will carry them through the day. I will often bring a friend a coffee for no particular reason, simply as a token of my love. My brother Suraj often says that he is "appreciative of my listening and attentive ear" and that he looks up to me as his role model because of it. It is important to me to provide that listening ear to those who need it because sometimes that is all that is necessary for a friend — to recognize the things that are good in his or her life. All of these moments are acknowledged with gratitude, for when we are filled with gratitude, we are always lighter and more hopeful in the moment.

We are all born with a spark of the divine, with joy, laughter and all of life's possibilities within us. Somewhere along the way, however, these magical assets become blanketed and often silenced by adult worries. What is so important for each of us to remember is those wonderful promises are still within us, waiting to be reignited by our divine power. Once we make the commitment to nurture and nourish this fire within, the engine that drives our soul purpose will once again allow us to attain significant levels of peace, serenity and wonder.

When we learn how to view our challenges as blessings, they often become the moments we remember most and treasure.

Happily, the very art of being grateful is now my fallback position whereby I can right my attitude before I slide into a negative state of mind.

"What you think, you become," says Buddha.

And so the power of positivity is an absolutely integral part of being grateful.

What I think I become: I am positive; I am grateful; I am full of appreciation and respect for everyone around me.

I encourage you to treasure all the milestones along life's path — those early days of struggling with career choices and decisions, the middle-of-the-night feedings and fever episodes when our children are babies. Many of us are also part of the sandwich generation, a time when we are run ragged with our careers, looking after our own families, and then also helping our aging parents. The gift of being there for our elders is a gift personified as we honour, respect and appreciate the sacrifices they made in their lives to help us get to an adulthood full of intention, loving relationships and friendships, while also being accountable members of our communities and good citizens of the world.

I want to share a story here about my friend Cecilia and her sister Carol Anne. The two sisters — barely 18 months apart in age — did everything together. They had an apartment together in their 20s where they threw celebrations for family and friends — really anyone who had anything to celebrate was on the sisters' radar. The sisters tried once or twice to throw surprise birthday parties for each other, but they were so intuitively connected that the one always knew what the other one was up to. The sisters took courses together and crafted homemade gourmet meals and handmade truffles, and they often showed up on each other's doorsteps with an item that the other had admired in a store that afternoon. Carol Anne introduced her sister to a colleague whom she taught with and whom Cecilia went on to marry, and then Cecilia returned the favour by introducing her to her husband's friend, who became Carol Anne's husband. Any friend of Cecilia's was a friend of Carol Anne's — and vice versa. The two were so inseparable that friends often called them the Siamese Twins. And so it is not hard to imagine the devastation when the sisters — who both shared the same doctor — were presented with the news that Carol Anne had stage 4 cancer and had mere months to live. With courageous hearts and devastated spirits, the sisters soldiered on, doing their best to make the most of their time together. Knowing that it was not the time to cave in to fear or grief, Cecilia put on a warrior face until she was behind her bedroom door, at which time a tsunami of tears would flow. When Carol Anne passed, friends, neighbours and colleagues waited in the two-hour lineup at the funeral parlour to pay their respects. Wondering exactly how she was going to put one foot in front of the other once the funeral was over, and with the loss of Carol Anne feeling both unbearable and unmanageable, Cecilia was at her wit's end until a good friend gifted her with a thought wrapped in gratitude that has kept my friend going through some particularly dark days.

"Weren't we all lucky to have her," the friend said to Cecilia as she hugged her tight.

It was an act of gratitude that lifted my friend up and gave her both faith and hope, because with the grace that is gratitude, we are often provided with resonant moments of hope and sustenance, a thin thread to hold onto until the next thread presents itself.

Being present in the moment with the people we are with — not just being physically present but mindfully present in thought and spirit — with no phone in hand or worry beads being recited around what happened that day or what's going to happen tomorrow — is the very essence of gratitude. Being present and available is the richest gift we can give to anyone.

"To stop and communicate with yourself is a revolutionary act," wrote the late poet, Buddhist monk, author and peace activist Thích Nhất Hanh. Being present in the moment, sitting quietly and just breathing in the gifts of the day, a practice sometimes called "mindful awareness," helps us to ground ourselves by being in ourselves – literally. The mind stops feeling lost and reconnects with our soul, our essence. Nhất Hanh urges us to put down our phones, turn off our computers, music or other distractions and instead listen to our breathing as we inhale in and exhale out, feeling our bodily sensations as our lungs and belly fill. He also encourages us to connect with the feelings that come from within and be open and responsive to following their direction.

He also recommends mindful walking as an effective way to bring together our bodies and minds, especially if it can be done in a natural setting.

"When you take a step with full awareness that you are taking a step on the ground and the Earth, there is no distinction between body and mind," he writes. Being present in the here and now means feeling how your body is connecting in the here and now with the Earth, our home, as you walk and breathe, see and hear, through your feet, breath, lungs, eyes and ears. These sensations are allowing you to connect with yourself, your body, your spirit and your feelings. He tells us to focus on our feet connecting with the ground. How difficult that simple task can be, though — we sometimes get so lost in our thinking that we don't know what's going on in our bodies, in our feelings or in the world around us.

"If you think while you walk, you're not really walking," he says. Instead, if you focus your attention on your breath and your step, being aware of the movement of your feet and the Earth beneath them, and repeat the mantra "I am home," you will free your mind from thoughts or worries of the past or the future. Here in your body and now in the present, you are home, he says — home and centred in the miracle that is your life. Practising mindful walking is one way we can remind ourselves of this truth.

The sharing of these practices has taught me that by being present in the moment and savouring the gifts of those moments, I am happy within myself and full of love. It is in those moments that I've learned to let go of the past and also to forgive myself for things that might be bothering me about that time. It's interesting what happens around regrets — often people don't know how to forgive themselves because they think that they are not worthy and don't deserve to be forgiven; they live in a state whereby they torture themselves with regrets.

But to what end? The past can be perceived as a negative or depressing time, while the future often causes anxiety. But when we allow ourselves to live in the present moment we become our best selves, and then we know that we are home. It is such a powerful and empowering state of being. The past is past; there is no purpose in replaying it with regret, which is such a painful and heavy emotion to carry around. The future is ours to create if we allow ourselves to do so. We can choose to live with the sadness and regret of the past or, as I tell myself: "I am here, I am in this moment, I am grateful, I am home."

The interesting lesson in all of this, as we acknowledge past transgressions and get to the point of forgiving ourselves, is that there is one more step that we need to take. We need to realize that as we change, transform and evolve, it is imperative that we let go of our pasts and make conscious decisions to not make those same mistakes again. It is then that we can move forward in gratitude, eager to embrace the magic that is happiness.

As Thích Nhất Hạnh said, "There is no way to happiness — happiness is the way."

In my gratitude practice, I have found that there are many moments when we either need to be helped or we need to be the source of help, a trusted warrior on whom downtrodden and distressed people can lean for strength, empathy and sanity. These are the moments when we learn from each other and live for each other's dreams and aspirations so that we can celebrate a life of positivity, generosity, love, caring and kindness together.

I am so thankful to God for allowing me to identify and actualize my soul purpose, which is the very essence of how I want to live my life.

When you work, you build a career.
When you give, you create purpose.
When you give a helping hand,
When you simply give a warm smile,
When you give to humanity, you receive love, abundance and magic.

When COVID-19 locked the world down, I could see that our employee member teams were frightened and fearful about what was going to happen next, both within their own family and social circles and, on a broader scale, about how the pandemic was going to affect the world at large.

Ever since I was a young child, I'd always felt that it was our duty as human beings and fellow citizens of the world to be kind to each other and to share what we had for the betterment of us all — but I was often told that I was too loving. When I espoused the concept that everyone deserved love, I was told that I was too naïve. But I am none of these things; rather, I am all of these things — I manifest love with a sincere and genuine heart. Some of the credit for my deep and genuine caring for others — especially those in need — goes to my parents. I remember that as a child, when I would find a dime, or a quarter, or a dollar in the street, my father would tell me that we needed to give it to someone who needed it much more than we did. Never were my siblings or I allowed to keep the money that we found.

And so my underlying thought has always been "If you have a love for God, how can you not have love for humanity?"

As such, as everyone struggled to adapt and make sense of the restrictions implemented to deal with the pandemic we were in, and because it has always been important to me to speak up and stand up for what I believe is right — with the purposeful intention of always doing my best to uplift humanity — I initiated a mission called *Project Kindness* as a way to help others and extend empathy and kindness. Within a very short time, and in conjunction with our staff's help, 1,870 pounds of food was donated to Second Harvest, a local Toronto food bank. Masks were dispatched to the University Health Network (UHN); 12.5 cases of place covers were shipped to a retirement home; and toiletries were donated to the City of Kingston Social Services. I also arranged to provide meals and snack-bag donations to Easton's Group of Hotels' members.

Through the Gupta Family Foundation, $336,462 was raised for "India Needs Our Help," money that was used to purchase concentrators to help the people living there to breathe.

I include this information not to in any way garner praise or fluff up my ego, but rather to show by example how helping others motivated and inspired me to nurture love, light and the ultimate values of faith and kindness in our valuable and highly respected employees. By its very name, *Project Kindness* became its own source of light, one that would impact on a local, national and international scale. As I have stated several times and cannot reiterate enough, I firmly believe that when challenges are put in front of us, they are wonderful and blessed opportunities for all of us to rise up to the occasion and create solutions that might otherwise have not been considered or explored.

And so, in partnership with Cornerstone Jamaica, the Gupta Family Foundation, led by me and my younger brother, Suraj, arranged to provide 400 ministry-approved tablets to students in need so that they could have access to and take advantage of greater educational opportunities for online learning during the ongoing COVID-19 pandemic. These tablets arrived on the #ContainerofLove, an initiative by @cornerstonejamaica to meet the needs of schools, organizations and communities in Hanover and Westmoreland, Jamaica.

My family's foundation is dedicated to spreading messages of hope and compassion because I am a firm believer that education is an asset that can't be taken away from a person — rather it can only grow and be shared. With education comes opportunity, and as a foundation, our mission and goals are to empower students through educational materials and assets.

Additional education initiatives were set up for children in Uganda and in Egypt. In the latter country, our foundation's mission was to economically empower the most impoverished and disadvantaged groups of women by providing them with the necessary skills to enter the labour market or microfinance training to enable and establish small businesses, thus providing the people in these countries with sustainable sources of income.

We also helped fund the MLSE Launchpad Programs, whose inherent purpose is to develop four key pillars: Healthy Body, Healthy Mind, Ready For School and Ready For Work.

As mentioned above, in February of 2023, my family foundation donated $100,000 to Global Medic, a Canadian-based charity that provides disaster relief in conflict and disaster zones. This particular effort was focused on areas of Turkey and its disenfranchised peoples and ethnic minorities. As part of these efforts, we recruited staff across the company to help Global Medic create aid kits that were shipped out to this country in crisis.

Throughout the company, and with all of our staff members,

I do my utmost to promote these mantras of love and gratitude:

Smile at a stranger.
Help those in need.
Speak your heart openly.
Give your love unconditionally.
When you love freely, you will attract love.
You will become love, and love will love you.

I have often been asked: “Reetu, why do you care so much about people?”

Simply put, I am who I am for one reason and one reason only, which is to speak love, action love, be love. From the time I was young, outsiders — who did not know or understand my soul purpose — would say to me: “Reetu, you are too nice, too caring, too helpful.”

But really, how can anyone be too much when it comes to love?

Whether it’s through philanthropic endeavours or work or when I’m just living my life, my mission and my soul purpose on Earth is to help, to serve humanity, to spread love, caring and kindness. So, if you think that’s weird, I am OK with that. I love and respect your opinion because you are you and I am me. We all have our path in life that we each need to follow.

In fact, my practice of gratitude fosters deep and open relationships with everyone I interact with throughout my day: family, friends, colleagues and staff at work. We all have so much to be thankful for. If we are lucky, we enjoy good health and are able to experience life robustly. So, take those moments throughout the day to close your eyes, release any negativity and quietly give thanks for what you are grateful for. Look around you and appreciate life’s little moments — a fresh cup of coffee; a glass of water clinking with ice cubes; a joyful friend; a success you have achieved at work; a bright flower blossom freshly picked; a child clapping her hands with glee as she swings high on the park swing.

Live your life where nothing is a miracle
or live whereby everything is a miracle.
Make it a point to see divinity in everything around you.

How do we do this?

Well, first of all, we have to be grateful for what we have, rather than envy what the next person owns. Too often we look at others and ask: "Why is she or he so successful? Why aren't I? Why haven't I attained that level of career success?" Sadly, social media has become an influence in so many of our lives, sparking moments of jealousy and feelings of negative self-worth for what others have and we don't. What many people don't realize is that the situations presented on social platforms such as Facebook, Instagram and TikTok are crafted scenarios that often don't have a shred of reality behind them.

We must stop comparing our lives and our life paths to others. We have to realize that we need to live our own lives with the soul purposes that have been gifted to us by the Universe. God has created a unique path for each one of us individually. God has dreams for us that are much bigger than our own. We each have the ability to access our own paths by having the faith and willingness to do so.

You can bring happiness into your life with faith in the Universe, faith in your Higher Power or God of your choice — ultimately, faith in the belief that you deserve to be happy and that you are worthy to be so. When we invest in our faith, we can be assured that we will actualize the soul purpose that has been created for each one of us on an individual basis.

Of course, we all have bad days — it is a natural result of being human. But the next time you feel down, the next time something happens that you find challenging or uncomfortable, give thanks for the lesson. In this moment, I ask you to perform an act of gratitude — a genuine act of appreciation and gratitude for the "what is" rather than the "what isn't." Because now you have your lesson, and God will bestow something great on you.

Things don't happen to us; they happen for us.

The disappointments that we experience prepare us for this state of gratitude. Nothing is wasted, not one single moment. When we adopt an attitude of gratitude, we develop trust, both in ourselves and in the Universe's oversight of us. Challenges strengthen us, they help build resilience, endurance and confidence within. As you move forward, every time you take a moment to say a quiet expression of gratitude, you are preparing yourself for life's next blessings. Bring faith into your life, not defeat.

In my practice, when I am in a state that is challenging or uncomfortable, I use the "I AM" affirmations to bring peace, serenity and gratitude to my situation, which allows me to invite blessings into my life.

I AM unleashing my power by speaking of gratitude and blessings.
I AM strong, resilient, and deserve positive blessings.

What we tell ourselves and what we put out into the Universe is what comes back to us — whether they be positive or negative results. Positive self-talk, positive speech and positive thought are akin to manifesting a form of karma. We can choose the karma we will manifest in our lives.

If you tell yourself, "I am tired, I am not good enough, I don't deserve it," then that becomes your reality. So instead, use strong, positive, affirmative-word statements:

"I am strong, I am worthy, I am energetic." This then becomes your truth.

Whatever we want our truth to be, we need to manifest it by speaking positively to those feelings. Gratitude has to come from the heart. It allows us to believe in ourselves; it empowers us to not only dream our dreams but to actualize them as well.

Being grateful also allows us to be open-hearted with our family and friends, which in my case means telling them on a constant basis that I love them. I show them I appreciate their love and friendship and support by writing them small notes of loving gratitude as well as buying them little presents that reflect their passions in life.

Science actually tells us that when gratitude is expressed and/or received, the brain releases dopamine and serotonin, two crucial neurotransmitters responsible for our emotions. Dopamine and serotonin contribute to feelings of pleasure, happiness and overall well-being.

How's that for the power of effective gratitude-giving!

As I've mentioned earlier in this chapter, grace is also a form of gratitude; if we can accept a situation or a person with grace, we then come to realize and understand that everything happens for a reason.

When my siblings and I were young, our Dad would gather us all in front of our temple first thing in the morning and have us say prayers of gratitude together. We would thank God for our family, for the roof over our head, for the food on our table and for the opportunities we would have that day to learn new things.

This practice of being grateful that my father instilled in us all was recently brought to the forefront by an unlikely but highly interesting source.

When I was in Grade 6 and, of course, having had gratitude ingrained in me so deeply, I wrote a note to the secretary at my school who had been remarkably kind to me after I fell in the schoolyard and ended up with a bloody knee.

In the letter I told this lovely woman what a good job she was doing typing and answering the phone (my note included a picture of her in a polka-dot dress doing exactly that!). I thanked her for telling me not to worry about the blood, that I was going to be all right, that it was not a big cut.

Thirty-three years have passed since that little girl wrote that letter of gratitude to someone who was so kind to her — and, in all honesty, I had totally forgotten about it until this woman died and her son found my note while going through his mother's things. And even though she would have nurtured thousands of children since that time, this woman saved my girlish printed note as a testament to the gratitude that lived in her own heart.

The Universe works in beautiful ways, and I ended up working alongside her son, Jeff. Her son had contacted me one day after he found the note and "knew it had to be the same Reetu," he told me. That he was so proud to share with me what effect my note had had on his mom was a reminder that my life's mission is to bring love into everything I do. I have found that when I treat people with love my ego becomes almost nonexistent.

If you don't have the gift of close family, embrace the supportive and trusted friends around you and treat them as your support structure. What I like to call my "Soul Family" doesn't have to be genetic.

The way that we attract our Soul Family is wrapped in simple acts of gratitude — what we put out into the Universe is what we attract back. If we *project kindness* and love, we will be paid back in kind.

I have been described as having a gentle, loving and accepting aura. It is what people receive because it is what I project. And so, I am often attracted to people who need the sustenance of kindness, tolerance, caring and a loving spirit — and they are attracted to me. But at the same time, I realize that people come into our lives for a reason and a season. Not everyone is destined to become a part of our Soul Family. Some people are with us for only a season, and it is our responsibility to make sure that their role is healthy and affirmative.

Gratitude is not just about counting our current blessings and saying a perfunctory thanks. Rather, it is about adopting the mindset of expressing our gratitude for all the blessings in our lives. And as a part of this, it is also important to bless the struggles as well as the gifts we enjoy.

In *The Book of Joy, Lasting Happiness in a Changing World* (Viking Books, 2016), author Douglas Abrams writes about a series of conversations that Nobel Peace Prize Laureates His Holiness the Dalai Lama and Archbishop Desmond Tutu conducted over 5 days as they discussed the question, "How do we find joy in the face of life's inevitable suffering?" Both agreed that the key to joy is to give love freely. We tend to be miserable when we are closed in on ourselves, the Archbishop observed. "It is in giving that we receive," he said. "When you give to others, it should be that you are subtracting from yourself," the Dalai Lama responded, laughing. "But, in fact, you are making space for more to be given to you," a strange arithmetic that doesn't seem to add up, but that is something we all know in our hearts to be true.

Having an open heart and sincerely supporting others on their journey will come back in kind to you. Being grateful for having a sense of humour and being able to laugh at my own mistakes helps me be open and receptive to my colleagues and staff.

In fact, whenever I engage in conversations with colleagues, I do my best to build real relationships and connections with them. They matter to me, which inspires me to perform little acts of gratitude to show them in a tangible way how much I love and respect them.

Another habit that brings me both great joy and peace is my gratitude journal, where I record the little unexpected gifts that have made my day that much richer and appreciative.

Acknowledging gratitude brings joy into our lives and allows us to see and appreciate the gifts that others bestow on us by their presence, friendship and love.

The action of practising gratitude in my life is the gifting to myself of mindfully thinking of three or four things that I am grateful for every day, a practice that keeps me rooted with and in positive energy. I say these acts of gratitude in a quiet space so that only my heart can hear them, and so that my soul intention can act on them. I like to give little mementos as reminders, things that I know mean something to the other person and which become reminders of gratitude.

I thoroughly enjoy buying little things for my younger brother and confidant, Suraj, as tangible reminders to him that I love him. We like to go away in the fall to a cottage up north, and so last year I bought him a stuffed Canadian moose to thank him for his support and for the way he uplifts me. He often tells me that I am his confidant because he knows that we intuitively connect in a way that allows me to be present for him at all times and that he can count on me to always have his back.

I have been described as selfless — my personal interests are way down on my priority list because others' needs in my Soul Family resonate as being my most important things to consider. As you read this you may wonder, "Does this thing called gratitude really work? Is it really worth me suspending my disbelief to try it?" my advice is to just try — but with an open mind and a genuine willingness.

Take a moment to consider what the positive outcomes of trying it might and could be, and then also consider whether you want to stay stuck in the cycle of negativity and inertia.

What have you got to lose?

At the end of the day, it's not what you might lose by embracing this endeavour, but what it is you might ultimately stand to gain in doing so.

And with that, I encourage you to speak, whisper, write, chant and sing your song of appreciation for the small and big moments of gratitude that the Universe gives you in this moment, this day, this book, with your family, friends and career.

Try this affirmation as you finish reading this chapter and discover how satiated your heart can be:

I am present.
I am joyful.
I am grateful.
I am motivated to help others, especially those in need. I believe in the vision that is my intuition, and I am confident in following that internal voice.
I am grateful that I have taken this time to read this book.
I am grateful and open to receiving the lessons and mind-opening possibilities presented within these pages.
I am open to receiving more lessons on gratitude, happiness and abundance.
I am going to continue embracing gratitude in my daily life.
I am open to the next possibilities that are presented in this book.
I am open at any age to the possibilities and opportunities that life presents.

I leave you with this quote from Maya Angelou, one that poignantly illustrates the joys of being present, being mindful and being grateful for "what is":

"A bird doesn't sing because it has an answer — it sings because it has a song."

CHAPTER 4

EMBRACING HABIT AND DISCIPLINE TO ACTUALIZE YOUR MOST AUSPICIOUS SOUL PURPOSE

"Change is life's responsibility;
transformation is our responsibility."

— Reetu Gupta

What is the first thing you think of when you hear the word "habit"?

How about "discipline"?

More often than not, one or both of these words will elicit little groans of "Oh, I have no self-discipline, especially when it comes to spending money on things I want, rather than things that I need," "I have a bad habit of eating junk food when I'm starving," or "I overdrink, especially when I'm at a party, or when I am upset or stressed." How about this: "I have a bad habit of staying up late on weeknights, binge-watching Netflix series while eating bowls of candy and chips"?

Human behaviour is such that it is easier to stay stuck in our current situation than it is to make the effort to change, which, in the bright glare of daylight, can feel like a Herculean effort.

Greek philosopher Aristotle said, "You are what you repeatedly do," and when we get stuck in a habit that does not serve us in a positive way, we eventually lose all power over it — unless we have the willingness to change how we look at the very things that are right in front of us.

Let me tell you a little story about a crab who was lost in his shell of negativity.

This little crab was an accomplished artist who made beautiful designs in the sand, intricate swirls that formed recognizable images such as maple leaves, stars and true-to-life flowers. Each time the crab finished a design, he would gaze upon them all and be overjoyed to see his creations carved into the luxurious sandy seashore. Then off he would go, scurrying into the water feeling ever so happy with what he had accomplished. However, one day, powerfully strong waves swept abruptly ashore and washed away all the crab's delicate designs. When the crab saw what had happened he was sad, angry and extremely disappointed.

"Why did you do that?" the crab shouted at the sea. "You are now my enemy because you have gone and washed away all of my magnificent designs, which I have spent so much time on."

The sea lovingly replied, "Mr. Crab, as I watched you roll into the sea, I saw a large predator fish swimming toward you and your family; he was coming straight for you. Your artwork is lovely but it left a clear map that would lead the predator fish directly to you and your family. I did what I did to save you."

In that moment, the crab realized that when we only focus on the negative, we fail to see the divine intervention. And while that reason may not be clear to any of us at first, it is important to stay centred in positivity and have faith in the outcome. We must believe that, behind the scenes, the Universe is championing "greater good" outcomes for all of us.

Staying committed to bad habits — mired in ones that not only keep us stuck but might also impact our mental and physical health — is aptly captured by Einstein's definition of insanity, which is doing the same things over and over again and expecting different results.

We promise ourselves that we will eat only healthily going forward or we will have only two drinks at the party. Maybe we promise ourselves that we will not go online and buy those "want-versus-need" items because we're bored or lonely and need an instant self-gratification bump. And when we focus on the negatives in our lives, counting other people's blessings instead of our own, we become discontented.

The first step to a positive feeling of well-being is changing how we view our circumstances and how we interact with ourselves. Self-talk can often be crafty and insidious as it weaves in negative thoughts and behaviours from our inner saboteurs, ones that we willingly latch onto in the absence of self-discipline. We need to take personal accountability for the kinds of outside influences that impact our thinking and that direct our thoughts in non-affirming ways. Owning how we choose to think and then choosing only those thoughts that best serve us is something that must become a conscious, self-directed, self-disciplined choice.

Compellingly, self-discipline, or the lack thereof, presents a fascinating topic in the study of human behaviour. We make personal promises to ourselves on an ongoing basis to do better in whatever area of improvement we've identified as needing change. We want to exercise more, eat less, eat better and spend better quality time with our family and friends. We want to save more, invest better, take courses, improve our career opportunities, begin a hobby or be kinder to ourselves.

As a means of justifying our human weaknesses, however, and to provide some encouragement to not be too hard on ourselves when we don't stick to our promises, it should be noted that there is scientific evidence to prove that when we indulge in things that turn us on like shopping, drinking, eating or gambling, our emotional brain, in the absence of a firm foundation of self-discipline, will choose cake over rice cakes or a slot machine rather than a savings deposit in order to get the instant blast of dopamine that comes from self-gratification. And therein lies the problem.

And while we might achieve partial success on our path to greater self-discipline, we often fail to envision how we are going to achieve our goals, as well as exactly how we are going to implement them.

So, how do we turn the negative practices that don't serve us well into ones that do?

For me, physically writing things down in an organized and concrete way helps me clarify what it is I want to achieve. Doing so also allows me to identify the steps I need to take to keep myself motivated and committed to action on a consistent and daily basis. Persistence, motivation and focus, coupled with strategies that I know will motivate me and resonate with my inner voice of discipline, have become part of my daily routine.

It can start with the simplest changes in our behaviour, ones that we commit ourselves to on a consistent and daily basis.

In his book *Be Exceptional* (Harper Collins Canada, 2021), Joe Navarro, a former FBI special agent, quoted some advice U.S. Navy admiral William H. McRaven, who'd been the commander of the U.S. Navy SEALs leading the raid on Osama bin Laden, gave to a group of students. McRaven had challenged them to guess the habits that might lead them to be exceptional leaders someday. How did McRaven know what qualities to foster in the young men and women under his command? Navarro quotes what McRaven told the students: "If you want to change the world, start off by making your bed." Research has shown that among the most reliable predictors of successful people is how conscientious and careful they are about fulfilling their smallest tasks, maybe even the most menial ones; by developing this habit, such people also develop a habitual sense of pride and self-worth. "Habitually bringing dedication to the small things we do each and every day creates a positive trend which, nourished properly, can become destiny," writes Navarro.

One of the disciplines that I've personally committed myself to on a daily basis for many years now — even on weekends and holidays — is the discipline of getting up each morning at 5 a.m. to meditate and set my intentions for the day. This time alone in silence, while it feels like the world is asleep, allows me to surround myself with divine light, cleanse my energy and surround myself with positivity, which ultimately impacts my day. It is my time to calm my mind and spirit in a loving, spiritual way as I reflect upon and then set my intentions for the day by aligning my passion, enthusiasm, thoughts, emotions and actions into one focused and disciplined approach.

Who we are today is a sum of the decisions and actions we took yesterday. And, so, who we will be tomorrow is based on the decisions and actions we take today.

As individuals, we each have the power to change our destinies, to create the kind of life paths that allow us to pursue our passions with love and light.

As part of that, when we choose our intentions each morning, we need to do so from a place that is centred in love.

Creating personal intentions is quite simple because, in their truest form, they stem from the deep desires, passions and dreams that live within our own hearts. Intentions come from that little voice inside us that has complete faith in the kind of person we can be. It is the voice that encourages us with love — for ourselves, for life and for others. When we have love, we have everything. It is also important for us to have faith in ourselves, for it is this trust that whispers to us that we are wonderful, that we are worthy to be loved, not just by others, but also by ourselves. It is this voice that inspires elite athletes to believe in themselves on their way to greatness and success. It is the voice that tells us that we are worthy and that we, too, can achieve our dreams. It is up to each one of us to awaken and empower our voices by creating our personal intentions.

I create my intentions by using positive wording and

affirmations because it is the words that we use and the truths that we tell ourselves that create the magic within. Because of that, we need to be specific with the wording that we choose. I focus solely on using positive wording to set my intentions. I stay away from saying things like "I can't" or "I won't."

For example, rather than say "I will not drink alcoholic beverages during the week," write your intention as an affirmative action: "This week, I will choose to enjoy alcohol only on the weekend and in moderation."

Replacing negative thoughts with positive statements effectively transforms what we hope to do into viable, achievable intentions.

Examples:

I will go the gym two times this week.
I will speak to my colleagues with patience and love.

When I am creating my daily intentions and setting my goals, there are three powerful, magical statements that I use on both a personal basis as well as when I am teaching meditation:

I am.
I can.
I will.

Some other personal affirmations that I use to set my intentions and which I am sure will be of help to you include:

I am love and light.
I will speak to myself with love.
I am deserving of love and will bring this love into my life.
I love my body and honour my body as it is. I will work to honour my body's health.
I am capable of achieving my goals.

I am capable of achieving my goals and dreams.
I go down this path with absolute confidence.
I will achieve my dreams.

Setting intentions in a clear, focused and loving way can transform what is sometimes considered the burdensome task of self-discipline into a practice that is easy to implement and actualize. I find that, when I meditate in the morning and give myself time for silence, my days are happier and lighter, and I can see the day ahead much more clearly. We will talk more about the benefits of meditation in Chapter 8.

Aristotle said that excellence is not an act; it is a habit. And when we make our habits, our habits make us — good or bad.

And when we include the discipline of good habits in our everyday lives, it leads to the actualization of our dreams. Each one of us has been gifted with our own unique story; we hold the pen and the power to write ourselves into our stories as loving, kind and inspirational heroes or heroines. The first step is simple: create habits that serve us well as individuals and be open and willing to embrace the personal discipline to live these habits.

Finding inspiration in people, places and things is also key to lifting me up in the process of achieving my personal goals. Almost every item that I surround myself with, from my clothing to my office to the walls of my condo, has reminders or elements of inspiration, positive energy and magic. For example, in my offices I keep a book of Rumi's poetry, a notebook that says "carpe diem" ("seize the day") and you will also find hearts and the word "love" everywhere. At my head office, I also keep a vintage Paymaster cheque-writer from the '80s, which lovingly reminds me of how far my family has come.

For example, today I am wearing yellow, a colour that ignites positivity and happiness in me. I am also wearing a costume jewelry ring, which is in the shape of a lotus, to remind myself that I can harness divine goddess power, and that in order for a lotus to bloom, its seed has to push through mud and water to reach the light of divinity.

One of my absolute favourite sources of inspiration is the Toronto Raptors basketball team. A squad with deep heart, the team inspires me on so many levels, to the point that every time I work out, I do so dressed from head to toe in Toronto Raptors clothing. When Nick Nurse published his book *Rapture: Fifteen Teams, Four Countries, One NBA Championship, and How to Find a Way to Win — Damn Near Anywhere* (Little, Brown and Company, 2020), I bought several copies for the leaders in my family's company because I found it to embody amazing leadership principles.

I also am blessed to own a signed jersey from former Toronto Raptors all-star forward #2, Kawhi Leonard.

What is it about Leonard that motivates me to include him in my sacrosanct inspiration corner, one where only the highest levels of achievement are recognized as standards of excellence to aspire to in my daily life?

In one word, silence.

In Game 7 of the Eastern Conference semifinals against the Philadelphia 76ers, against untold pressure and a packed arena of shouting fans, Leonard paused for that all-important brief moment of silence before taking the game-winning shot that has since earned its place in NBA folklore. In fact, that shot cemented the Toronto Raptors' place in the Eastern Conference finals, on their way to their successful win of the 2019 NBA Championship. As he watched the ball hit the rim a total of four times, Leonard sat silent and emotionless, crouched on the heels of his running shoes as he silently waited (and in my opinion, was in meditation) for the ball to drop through the basket. It was only after the ball finally dropped that Leonard jumped up and let out what was an uncharacteristic scream, relief and joy showing in every muscle of his face.

It is an image that I embrace in my everyday life as I rise at dawn to meditate and pray. As the Persian Sufi mystic and poet Rumi said: "The dawn breeze has secrets to tell you, don't go back to sleep."

To hear these secrets, we must be silent, focused and willing to receive.

Silence in and of itself is a renewing source of strength, one that, when we use it to stop the chatter from within, can become one of our greatest reserves of serenity.

"Modern humans have lost touch with their inner 'true self,'" notes Steve Taylor, an esteemed author and lecturer on spirituality and psychology, who argues that silence and stillness, which are the tools we can use to recover that true self, happiness and contentment, have almost completely ceased to exist in our modern world. Because people are no longer used to silence or inactivity, they have become afraid of being quiet and still, and are determined to avoid silence and inactivity at all costs. Being confronted with either unnerves them. But we need silence and stillness to become our true selves and to be truly happy. "Be still and know that I am God," said Jesus. But "he might have added, 'and know that you are God,'" Taylor observes in his essay "The Power of Silence" *(https://www.stevetaylor.com/essays/the-power-of-silence).*

Silence is centring; it separates us from the white noise that surrounds us, and it gifts us with the ability to gather our thoughts and power our next steps toward realizing our goals.

In a *Washington Post* article the day after his famous buzzer beater, Leonard is quoted as saying: "I didn't want to leave any shots in my mind. I wanted to leave it all on the floor. This could have been my last game for the season. I would have had to wait five months to put up another shot in a game. I wasn't going to worry about makes or misses, just tried to will us to a win."

Another moving example of the power of discipline actualized is the story of Olympic gold medalist Muhammad Ali and his journey to greatness. Born Cassius Clay Jr. in Louisville,

Kentucky, in 1942, to Cassius Marcellus Clay Sr. and Odessa Grady Clay, whose ancestors had been slaves for six generations, Muhammad Ali's childhood was wrapped in strife.

Segregation was rife in the southern United States at that time and, to add to the stress, the young boxer, who began his training at 12 years of age, also struggled with dyslexia, barely managing to graduate high school.

The story of how Ali got his start has been retold umpteen times. After pedalling on his brand-new bike to a fair in his hometown of Louisville, he left the bike outside a venue while he went in to see a show, but when he came out the bike was gone. He sought out a police officer and told him that his bike had been stolen and that when he found the person who took it he was going to beat him up. Serendipitously, Joe Martin, the police officer, was a trainer at a local gym, and he offered to give the boy some boxing lessons.

It was the direction he needed, one that propelled the young Clay forward on the arduous path that with determination and discipline became his life's destiny. Famous for his outsized and memorable boasts — "Float like a butterfly, sting like a bee" and "I am the greatest!" — he was known to jump rope for hours on end to strengthen his legs. He also practised in front of mirrors to improve his reflexes and boost his confidence.

In 1960, six years after he began his training, Clay Jr. won Olympic gold in the light-heavyweight division against the Polish contender Zbigniew Pietrzykowski.

When he converted to Islam in 1964, officially changing his name to Muhammad Ali, the young boxer's belief in himself was such that he refused to buckle under the subsequent public, political and religious hue and cry. And rather than answering the United States military draft call to fight in the Vietnam War in 1966, Ali became a conscientious objector, which resulted in him being sentenced to five years in prison (Ali did not end up serving any time in prison), a $10,000 fine and the revoking of his passport. Stripped of his boxing title and banned from the ring for three years, Ali's comeback was spectacular. Between 1964 and 1978, he won 56 of his 59 boxing matches. Inducted into the International Boxing Hall of Fame in 1990, Ali was also awarded the U.S. Presidential Medal of Freedom in 2005.

Undeterred, self-disciplined and full of an unshakeable belief in himself that did not entertain naysayers, Ali did not forget his roots. Along with his wife, Lonnie Ali, he championed literacy for African-Americans and created *Go the Distance*, a series of books and magazines specifically chosen to inspire and motivate Black readers.

Now while it is a good habit to be mindful and open to the Universe's messages and empathetic to other people's circumstances within our circles, we also need to be aware of people's insecurities and jealousies and how their foibles, anxieties and deep-seated fears too often insert themselves into our own personal lives, presenting as mean-spirited and judgmental criticism.

In *The Four Agreements*, Don Miguel Ruiz advises us to not take things personally. He notes that when we feel offended by something someone has said to us, our first reaction is to defend our beliefs and attack the person who has offended them — that is, challenged our deepest sense of self. "Because you have the need to be right and make everybody else wrong, you make something big out of something so little," Ruiz observes. But the struggle to have your own opinions prevail over theirs is usually futile, and the conflict just leaves us vulnerable to other people's issues, he says. When you can make it a habit not to take anything personally, the anger, jealousy, envy and sadness provoked by such conflicts will disappear, he writes.

Making this personal agreement a habit — a written pact that we make with ourselves so that our heart sees what our mind has written — will negate other people's negativity, jealousies and insecurities, which in turn will not allow our serenity to be compromised.

I put this fourth agreement into practice several years ago, because my life choices of rising early, meditating, not drinking alcohol and being vegan affected the way people treated me and often resulted in their judging me. Peer pressure is a powerful force, but I put that negative social chatter aside because the choices I decided to make for myself were ones that ultimately reflected my morals, my values, my integrity and, most importantly to me, my spirituality.

Of course, some of the main pitfalls that I am sure we can all relate to as we try to become more self-disciplined are the excuses that we tend to tell ourselves when the "going" gets too tough.

In *Excuses Begone!: How to Change Lifelong, Self-Defeating Thinking Habits* (Hay House Inc., 2011), Dr. Wayne W. Dyer talks about the influence the eminent master Lao-Tzu had on his thinking, allowing his thoughts to clarify and harmonize with his higher self. Dyer describes how to change life-long habits of thinking by asking ourselves seven questions about the excuses we tell ourselves to avoid change:

Is this excuse true? Where did it come from in the first place? What do I gain by believing it? What would my life look like if I couldn't use this excuse? Is there a reason to change? Will my support network help me to shed old habits? How will I be able to continuously reinforce my new way of being?

When you carefully examine the explanations you make to yourself, it may dawn on you that what you've been telling yourself may not be true at all, Dyer writes, "yet even though they're lies, they do bring some sort of reward," he adds.

Dyer also notes that the ways we think about our own self-worth and worthiness of being loved were often planted in us as children and have been based on what others thought of us, on being popular, on being well-behaved, on being "good," on winning or performing well. Those beliefs, seeded in us as children, can be very deeply rooted in us as adults, so that our self-worth hangs on what others think of us. But their assessments so often hang on what they see or what we have, our possessions or our appearance, not who we really are.

As my spirituality evolved and my dedication to meditating on a daily basis became an integral part of who I am, I became more mindful of the things I was putting into my body and how they affected my overall health. As I focused on becoming the best version of myself, I chose to go vegan, which at the time was a very uncommon choice. I also decided to abstain from drinking alcohol. I have not always lived this way, and while my mother has never eaten meat or drunk alcohol, she was open to my brother and I making our own decisions. As such, I also encourage my friends and those around me to eat what lifts them up, what feeds their soul, their physical and mental health and, ultimately, their spirit. Living well and in spiritual light is the ultimate actualization of self-discipline for me.

But choosing to go vegan and to give up alcohol, especially, were not easy decisions for me. As far as alcohol goes, my decision to abstain from drinking came about because I felt it no longer suited my aspirational lifestyle. It was a life choice that was met with a lot of drama and negative feedback from my friends. But I decided it no longer served me to put a substance into my body that did not enhance my physical, mental or spiritual well-being. However, the reaction from my community was as if I had just announced that I was becoming a yogi and moving to a distant forest or monastery, where I would be locked up with no further interaction with the outside world. The questions friends asked me were bizarre:

"Surely you will have one drink with me, at least?"

"You will have a drink on special occasions, though, right?"

"Having a glass of wine doesn't count — it's just grapes, after all."

It is interesting that at a very young age I was empowered to make a promise to myself that I would never make a decision that would compromise my integrity. I hold myself to a high standard and have always done so. After all, I am the one who needs to feel good, and I could decide to satisfy friends and loved ones, but, at the end of the day, it is me that needs to be happy and comfortable with my choices. I have chosen to abstain from drugs, and I continue to honour that decision. When I was growing up and in middle school, the group of girls I hung out with started experimenting with marijuana. I was not comfortable with what they were doing and I had to make a choice. These girls were lovely, but I just did not want to spend my spare time indulging in habits that I was not open to nor comfortable with. I decided to take a step back from those girls, which resulted in me having no friends for a while — a tough outcome at that age, as you can imagine. But it was my decision to make. It's not that I judged these girls or looked at what they were doing as being morally wrong. Rather I looked at it as not wanting to put drugs into my body and exposing me to a decision that I did not want to make.

Because removing alcohol from my life was a conscious decision that I made to elevate myself on my way to a more spiritual life, I am able to accept the questions and noise that sometimes comes from me not drinking. I actually find it rather amusing to be at corporate functions and observe people and their reactions when I say I don't drink. Not drinking also gives me the opportunity to people-watch in social settings, which is something that I love to do; I learn so much from just watching. People truly reveal themselves when you pay close attention.

I've found that society does not embrace discipline, but rather, it embraces a lifestyle where fun is the ultimate, romantic way to live. And I am OK with that. Each one of us chooses to live our lives in a way that best suits our heart force. Personally, I am here to honour my intentions to live my life in a meaningful and purposeful manner, which includes a daily commitment to meditation, silence and affirmative behaviour.

And while some people do not find discipline until later in life, for others it is almost innate. I consider myself lucky to have been born with a level of discipline that is unusual for most kids. Even as a youngster, I would set my own alarm to get up and get ready for school. And although I attended kindergarten at a Montessori school where I learned at my own speed, I am inclined to think that my discipline is somehow genetic, not a learned behaviour. Even at that young age, I would come home from school, take off my clothes, fold them and put them away neatly. My parents taught my brother and me the importance of establishing goals and working toward actualizing them.

Because the spirit is willing but the flesh is weak, I find that it is non-negotiable that I stick to my consistent routine. Discipline is hard. It is a habit that for some people comes easy, but for others is almost impossible to implement. The days that I don't follow my morning practice and routines are the days that I find myself less centred, less focused and less me.

The discipline of habit and the habit of discipline, once embraced and actualized in our daily lives, are practices that will bring continued joy, contentment, serenity and the kind of positive spirit that will light up those around us.

As we explore our practice together and embrace the personal habits that will allow us to live a happier, more disciplined lifestyle, I am happy to share with you the three definitive attributes that keep me centred and disciplined in my everyday practices. These are courage, conviction and confidence.

I wish and gift all three of these to you on your path to a more meaningful and self-disciplined life.

As Paulo Coelho has written, "*a yes or no could change your whole life*."

CHAPTER 5

BELIEVING IN YOURSELF TO BECOME YOUR MOST AUTHENTIC YOU

"I can choose either to be a victim of the world or an adventurer in search of treasure. You are what you believe yourself to be."

— Paulo Coelho

It is a simple thing, really. Or at least it should be — the all-encompassing emotional, spiritual and physical practice of believing in ourselves. To not do so seems almost bizarre because who else are we with 24/7 besides our very own selves?

If I were to pause here for a moment and ask you if you honestly believe in yourself, if you are self-loving and living your most authentic self, one that actualizes your joy, passion and soul purpose in life, what would your answer be?

I ask this question not out of any sense of judgment or self-shaming, but rather out of a sincere and passionate desire to help you pursue your passions in life, whatever they may be. Along my life's journey, I have found that, rather than being overwhelmed at where I am, where I am not, or where I think I should be, it serves me well when I change my mindset to encompass this four-word mantra: Begin where you are.

It is from this point that I can allow myself to move forward with a positive mindset and spirit to actualize my most fervent goals.

One of the extenuating circumstances that I have heard many people identify as being a fundamental setback in their adult lives is that somewhere along the line they were told, or have told themselves, that they are less than, not worthy of being the most authentic, self-confident version of who they aspire to be. Interestingly, while we have absorbed some of these non-serving feelings and thoughts in adulthood, many of these negative messages have also been ingrained in us from childhood. There is no denying that, for many of us, our experiences as children shaped and impacted our beliefs and our impressions about ourselves. I grew up with parents who showed my siblings and me by example what a loving, supportive kind relationship and environment looked like. We absorbed and attached our self-worth growing up based on the figureheads in our lives — whether that was positive or negative. Kindness tends to foster kindness; non-affirming circumstances, however, have the ability to create deep trauma unless we can find the strength to overcome it.

If as children we were protected in such a way that did not allow us to have certain new experiences because of all the risks associated with them, now as adults our fearful and impressionable minds suggest to us that it is not OK to put ourselves out there to try the very things that enhance our mettle and deepen our resilience.

Too often, overprotective parents do not allow their children to "fail forward" because they are afraid of the emotional impact that it will have on their child. Interestingly, however, it is in the very acts of "falling down seven times, getting up eight" that our success rate as adults is actualized.

In *The Book of Joy*, Archbishop Desmond Tutu observes that the Dalai Lama's serenity, calm and joyfulness might be the result of all the adversity that he has gone through, not in spite of that adversity.

For us, as well, it is important to sit with our childhood memories and, with a loving spirit, both honour those early influences that have shaped us in a positive way and at the same time examine the negative things that we absorbed so that we can honestly assess the validity today of those beliefs. Our sense of personal self-worth needs to be nurtured from within and not be dependent on what others think of us.

"As adults, part of our self-love journey is to unearth the parts of ourselves we buried, form beliefs that are aligned with our values, and cultivate an environment that's safe for us to be authentic," which will allow us to be loved unconditionally by others and, most importantly, by ourselves, says Mary Jelkovsky in 100 *Days of Self-Love, A Guided Journal* (Blue Star Press, 2022).

When we do the work and recognize that no matter what, who we are is enough, that we have as much right as the next person to be our most authentic selves, our self-esteem then becomes the light to guide us along our journey. And, rather than take for granted the positive guidance and feedback I received as a child, I make it a point to be grateful to my mother and father and honour the gift of self-worth that they instilled in me.

As a young girl, I would often seek out my mom's advice, especially as it related to my fashion choices. I remember, on one occasion, feeling a bit shy about what I was planning to wear to a family event. I had on what I considered the right amount of "bling," but I knew other people might think that my look was "too much." Because I was not even a teenager at that point, I remember being vulnerable to other people's opinions, but when I went into my mom's room to ask her how I looked, she said: "*Beta* (which is Hindi for "daughter"), you look perfect, absolutely beautiful. I want you to walk into the party and onto the dance floor and not care for one second what people think!"

These words echoed in my mind and became a symbol for how I would behave in life: that no matter what I do, I should always walk with my head held high and smile as if I am a lead actress on the stage of life. Her words of support truly gave me confidence and faith in my identity.

But how do you do this — get to that place where you feel comfortable in your own skin and humbly proud of yourself when you look in the mirror?

I believe it all starts with having the courage to look at your reflection and say "I Love You." Having the courage to tell yourself you have had a hard journey but you are here, and to remind yourself that the decisions you make today can affect your tomorrow. You get to decide who you want to be!

Another way is with willingness to change and allowing yourself to look at situations through a different set of lenses — and with a different attitude. If I welcome a challenging situation with enthusiasm and confidence rather than fear and impatience, I am amazed at how much quicker a solution presents itself to me. And when I consciously embrace joy and am able to laugh at myself, it robs the saboteur of its influence and power, gifting me instead with a strong sense of self-worth and belief in myself. When we value ourselves and set non-negotiable boundaries, our stock in ourselves rises as our character defects are tabled and then subsequently resolved. The stalemates in our lives that are often defined by the words "if," "and," "but" and "cannot" become moot in the face of joy and light in our hearts.

We also have to look at and decide how we are going to deal with fear, which is an amazingly powerful emotion that can be either a natural phenomenon or one that contagiously embeds itself into our very beings through transmission from others who do not want to see us succeed and thrive. In fact, I feel so strongly about the impact that fear can have on a person's life that I have changed what is often a common acronym — and which you have already heard me mention previously in this book, Fear

Everything and Run, to Face Everything and Rise. I manifest this saying with what is now a familiar affirmation to you:

I am.
I can.
I will.

The words, the very narratives that we speak to ourselves, have the power to create our personal destinies. They are the engines with the wherewithal to transform not only our own lives, but those around us as well.

If a voice tells you "You cannot, you are not, you will not," then it is up to each one of us to run that voice off, write that voice right out of our very psyche.

It is of utmost importance to remember that we all go through difficult times; no one goes untouched. But it almost feels sometimes that we are being tested by the all-encompassing Universe. I do not believe, however, that God is ever testing us; rather, I believe that He puts challenges in front of us that He knows we can handle and can conquer. He does not give us more than we can handle. He gives us the free will and the power to believe in ourselves as a means to honouring ourselves and our purpose in life. Rather than tests, I believe life's challenges are a testament to God's love and belief in us.

But human nature is such that even if we have eight or nine or ten skills that we are highly accomplished at, we will nonetheless return again and again to the one or two things for which we don't have a particular talent.

It is critically important to keep in mind that we are all gifted with both strengths and weaknesses. When we believe in ourselves, we are doing just that — believing and having faith in our own abilities.

Unbridled faith gives us the confidence to overcome self-doubt, fear and the kind of self-sabotaging actions that push us down to disempower us.

"Every human mind is fertile, but only for those kinds of seeds it is prepared for," says Ruiz in his book *The Four Agreements.* "What is important is to see which kind of seeds our mind is fertile for, and to prepare it to receive the seeds of love." When hurtful things were said to us by our parents and siblings when we were children, those words were most likely expressed thoughtlessly in frustration or anger, with no understanding of the long-term negative impact they would go on to have on our young impressionable minds.

No matter how old we are, if we have not done the work to elevate ourselves, we tend to take these criticisms to heart and carry them around with us in our subconscious; before we know it, we are regurgitating negativity from childhood. And so, as Ruiz instructs in *The Four Agreements*, our words to others, and especially those we tell ourselves, need to be "impeccable" – that is, faultless.

Of course, as human beings, we sometimes can't help questioning the situation. We ask: Why me? Why not her? Why is she or he happy and I'm not?

But all that negative energy can be very time-consuming, both spiritually and emotionally. In these moments, I want you all to remember that each one of you has your own path to follow, your own lessons to learn.

When we recognize that it is possible to change the negative perceptions we have about ourselves, we can then shift our state of mind to a place that is centred in self-worth and confidence.

I find that when I am faced with a situation that is challenging or feels uncomfortable, rather than slip into old thinking, I pause and take the time to reflect and meditate on how my most powerful self would handle it.

As author Carol Louisa Gawain, whose nickname was Shakti (the Sanskrit word for the divine feminine creative force) observed, "Every time you don't follow your inner guidance, you feel a loss of energy, loss of power, a sense of spiritual sadness."

And so, if I am in a difficult situation, I turn to the values and tenets that I have built my confidence and self-belief upon, which in turn helps me look squarely at the issue with confidence and empowerment. Rather than turn away from the voice of fear, the inner saboteur that loves to present itself in stressful situations, I turn to my faith in the Universe, in my inherent belief that the Universe will conspire to make it happen, when I want something badly enough.

We all go through the pains of living life on life's terms, but we can choose not to suffer. Instead, when we believe in ourselves and our own inner strength, fortitude and resilience, the courage to make it through the darkness becomes our way into the light. I encourage you with full heart to never give up. Even when it feels like others have given up on you, do not give up on yourself. Personal strength comes not from what you can do, but from overcoming the things you once thought you could not. It is a fact that we never know how strong we are or how strong we can be until strength is the only choice we have. When we believe in ourselves, the world listens and will manifest that belief. Courage does not always appear as a roaring voice, but rather the quiet voice at the end of the day that says, "I will try again tomorrow."

Being authentic, being yourself and living in your truth takes courage; it takes bravery. For me, the LGBTQSIA community is the most authentic and strongest community because they stand so strongly in their truth, despite all the barriers and challenges against them. This beautiful community not only takes pride in their identity, they celebrate it. It is a notion we can all learn from and is so incredibly inspiring to me!

And so, when others are trying to impart their opinion or will on me, a force of intimidation that attempts to push me down rather than lift me up, I repeat this powerful affirmation to myself and wait until my personal sense of empowerment returns.

I am strong.
I am confident.
I am here for a reason that is unique to me.
I am courage, conviction, confidence.
I embrace change and am grateful for its transformation, its manifestation in my life.
I let go and let God.
I allow my light to shine through.
I AM.
I CAN.
I WILL.

I am grateful for what is, where I have come from and what is possible today.

As Rumi advised, "Respond to every call that excites your spirit. Ignore those that make you fearful and sad, that degrade you back toward disease and death."

As an example of how I have manifested my belief in self, I will share with you my experiences around being a model. I have always had a passion for fashion — in fact, I still do, and so when I was in my early 20s, I took up modelling. It wasn't long, however, before I realized that this was a profession that was not in sync with my morals and values. I would hear representatives at the modelling agencies saying things like "She's too Indian; she's not Indian enough; I need a 34B cup, not a 36C; she has to be 5 foot 9, not 5 foot 7."

There was actually one fashion show that I was working — we were not told ahead of time what we were modelling — and the designer asked me to wear a bikini. I refused to wear it even though I was fully cognizant of the fact that my decision might get me thrown out. The designer ended up putting me in another outfit, which I was grateful for. But I decided right then and there that I would never make a decision that would compromise my integrity or my self-respect. I feel that I would rather walk away and know that I had respected my beliefs — my belief in who I am and what I felt comfortable doing — than to cave into someone else's wishes.

Simply put, my decision was a purposeful manifestation that honoured my authenticity, a conscious action of being true to my own self, my values and spirit, regardless of the pressure I was under. It was an honest and aware alignment of the ideals that are an integral part of my soul purpose. Believing in myself wholeheartedly allows me to be my most authentic self. I am honest in my acknowledgement around what I am not good at, but I am also unapologetic around what I am good at, what I know in my heart that I have a passion for and excel at. This does not come from a place of ego, but rather, an honest and faithful belief in myself. When we have a clear and realistic idea of what our capabilities are, it allows us to create and build a better plan relative to what steps need to be taken to actualize our dreams, which in turn manifests our soul purpose. That unshakeable confidence in ourselves, one that is not shifted or shaken by outside criticisms and jealousies, is the very definition of self-empowerment.

We need to push out of our comfort zone so that we can discover our own capabilities, our own sense of self-worth, and self-confidence, which is born out of achieving our aspirational goals.

There are many challenges on this journey, including the fact that we are prone to comparing ourselves to others — not to mention that as we age, we compare ourselves to younger versions of ourselves — and the trap for the entanglement of negative self-worth and low self-esteem is set.

As such, recognizing the fact that who we are is a notion that we create, so we can embrace the steps toward how we can change our feelings and behaviours into a flag-waving parade of self-belief and robust acceptance.

Doing the work every day to lift myself up and out of non-serving places, ones born out of false childhood memories or petty jealousies or just plain thoughtlessness, I begin each day with a loving and positive affirmation to myself, which in turn seeds my day with the mirror image of who I envision myself to be, the authentic spiritual me that espouses love each time I sit in silence as I check in with myself. It is the faith in self that knows no bounds.

There are times when even though we have achieved a notable level of success, our belief in our authentic selves is sabotaged by imposter-syndrome thinking, which is rooted in a sense of fear that we are not good enough, not deserving enough, not capable enough to flourish in the situation we've worked so hard to achieve.

It is imperative to remind ourselves each and every day that it is critical to invest and embed high levels of trust in ourselves. We also have to remember that it is important to be open-minded and receptive to the Universe's message and be confident that the signs that come to us are there for us to acknowledge and use on our journey to a positive and successful life.

Once we recognize that the pursuit of our passions and the successful execution of them are our reasons for being and our soul purpose in life, we should not be afraid of where our next great idea will take us. Nor should we be afraid that when we arrive at that crossroad, we will be ready and able to move forward, as long as we are willing to stay true to our authentic selves.

"If you base your self-worth on what everyone else thinks of you," that is, something you have no control over, "you hand all your power over to other people and become dependent on a source outside of yourself for validation," writes author Jen Sincero in *You Are a Badass: How to Stop Doubting Your Greatness and Start Living an Awesome Life* (Running Press Adult, 2020).

"What you seek,
Is seeking you"
-Rumi

When we listen to words and choose to follow our heart's calling, our hearts will whisper our destiny to us. We will see our path unfold on our way to achieving what we desire.

So, what does it mean to be your authentic self, and how do you go about faithfully actualizing your most faithful and genuine version of yourself?

Well, for me, it means making it a non-negotiable priority to start my day with gratitude and positivity. If I tell myself first thing in the morning that "I have a stressful day ahead" or "I am so tired" or "I am not looking forward to dealing with that difficult person at work today, I hate my work," that is exactly how my day will evolve, with that negativity.

However — and this is an unequivocal and proven fact, one that I can personally attest to — when I greet the day with gratitude, enthusiasm and light, I manifest the very things that I want to do on a consistent and empathetic basis. What we think is what sets our intentions and is ultimately what the Universe manifests.

So instead of saying "I am stressed" or "I am tired" or "I am irritable and discontent" — thoughts that can and will direct the course of our day — I encourage you to change your mindset to manifest "I am happy; I will get what I need, at the right time and in the right way."

Other short and positive affirmations that you can easily include throughout the day to keep yourself centred and focused include:

I am here.
I am mindful.
I am happy.
I am inspired.

I am.
I can.
I will.

Realizing that you can count on the God of your understanding to give you exactly what you need today and every day are the rungs on the ladder of gratitude, happiness and content. It is this kind of preparation, when done on a consistent basis, that will allow you to trust and appreciate your singular purpose in life. Just as there are no two snowflakes alike in the Universe, so too there are no two people exactly alike. We are each here to actualize a soul purpose that is completely unique to us.

Live life *with* happiness, not *for* happiness. If you tell yourself "I will be happy once I get this job, or when I get this house, or that relationship," you are putting conditions on your happiness. In fact, what we are effectively doing when we engage in this kind of thinking is that we are wasting the promise of today for the promise of what *might* be tomorrow. But if we allow ourselves to be happy in the present as we work toward achieving our goals, we will attain the keys to happiness, self-fulfillment and serenity.

I cannot say it enough: Live life *with* happiness, not for happiness.

To do this, I faithfully practise being kind to myself. I give myself the benefit of the doubt rather than second guessing or judging my decisions. I have learned not to compare myself to others on a physical, emotional or financial basis.

If you are working with someone else on either a personal or professional basis, find your common interests and goals, your common missions, values and purpose, so that your authentic selves can complement and actualize each other's soul purpose.

One of the most effective and clearest paths to understanding who we perceive and want our most authentic selves to be is to do the hard work of being honest, open and realistic about what and who our authentic self really is. First — and yes, I am once again recommending that you apply this disciplined habit to your practice — put pen to paper and start writing with an open and quiet heart what your authentic self looks like to you — the traits and values, the abilities and wonderful personality traits that define your most magnificent self.

Believe that each day brings a miracle of its own and, because it does, we need to be grateful for the little things that surround us — the friendships, the spring flowers that poke their determined heads out of the newly thawed soil after a harsh winter, the bountiful food that fills our cupboards, the freshly poured coffee or the Beaujolais wine chilling in our fridge, just waiting to be opened in celebration and joy.

"When you want something, all the universe conspires in helping you to achieve it," as Coelho writes in *The Alchemist*. In fact, many of Coelho's lessons highlight the importance of coming to the realization that we should never allow anyone else to be responsible for how we feel, and that we are what we truly believe ourselves to be.

And so, what are some of the ways that we can breathe life and purpose into the mind-filled actions that define an innate belief in ourselves?

Well, I have to admit that there are times when I take myself very seriously and, in those times, I am as strong as thunder when it involves my morals and integrity. I will not allow anyone or anything to compromise these tenets. That being said, I love to smile and I love to laugh any chance I get. In fact, I make it a point to create situations so that laughter and a "touch of magic" surround me. As mentioned, I am an ardent Toronto Raptors fan and I go out of my way to watch them, attending home-court games whenever possible. This simple passion has allowed me to nurture friendships with like-minded people who I've just met for whom the team also brings great joy, enthusiasm and outsized, dedicated cheering. Joyous activities heal our souls and are a wonderful prescription for the ailments of life. I believe in myself and the skills and abilities that I have worked so hard to achieve, to the point that I am now easily able (most of the time, anyway!) to laugh at my own mistakes. And you know that person you see laughing in the car beside you in rush hour traffic? Guess what! It could very likely be me laughing to myself as I remember something funny or ridiculous that happened to me five years ago. It is indeed important to find the joys in life, even in the hardest of times. Find a reason to smile or find a reason to make someone else smile. I am often told by others that I am always smiling, that I am always joyful. I attribute this to my connection with the Universe and the faith that I am exactly where I need to be, who I need and want to be. Why wouldn't I smile when I am immersed in such joy and gratitude?

When we become adults, we often forget the magic and joy of being children. We should be mindful of this and not let go of this unbridled joy because it is what keeps us young. In fact, it can become our effective suit of armour to alleviate life's stresses and worries.

In order to respect ourselves and honour our soul purpose, it is also important that we set boundaries with people who take our time for granted, who deplete our energy resources by their negativity and pessimistic approach to life, which is not to say that we should be unavailable for cherished family members and loyal friends. But when helping others becomes an ongoing process of manipulation and enabling, it is time to set the kinds of parameters that protect our personal warrior boundaries and badges.

It is also good to set aside some non-negotiable time for ourselves to do the following: sit in silence to meditate and reflect on the day's blessings; journal in a notebook about our heartfelt experiences of smell, feel and beauty; sit outside on a warm summer evening and listen to the birds sing their nightly song of gratitude for their found worms and their magnificent wings; take a solitary walk in nature and listen to what our fellow beings have to say — the crickets, the streams and even the silent breath of the trees. There is a magic to the mundane, a glorious celebration to be found in the spectacular purple, reds, blues and yellows of wildflowers that grow along the country roadside.

An affirmation to empower our day involves two of the most powerful words in the Universe which, combined with actionable verbs, will and can change the direction of our day. For whatever words follow, I AM is what we manifest in our lives. Spoken aloud in a quiet space, these purposeful action-based intentions will manifest your destiny and breathe purposeful focus into your daily life.

I AM.
I CAN.
I WILL.
I am powerful.
I am creative.
I am happy.
I am inspired.
I live life with happiness.
I smile more often and in more situations.
When I smile, God and the universe smiles with me.
I have the ability to manifest my desires.

It is also important to have faith in ourselves and to listen to our hearts. Our Higher Powers exist within us, and it is our ultimate faith in self and the Universe that allows us to see the path forward with confidence and trust. When we consciously practise this connection to and with our hearts, we are preparing ourselves for the difficult times when we need to access these "faith-based premiums" as a way to guiding ourselves forward in hope and light.

Remember when you are in the midst of taxing or difficult times to know that, in spite of and because of them, you will come out the other side with strength, resilience and enhanced empathy. By doing the work on a daily basis, by being impeccable with your words and your support of self, you will be prepared and ready to live life on life's terms. You are walking the path and actualizing your soul purpose.

Start your day with positivity, with the people and things in your life for which you are grateful and make you whole. Use your morning affirmations as your subconscious engines for the day: I am energetic; I look forward to actualizing my day with a grateful and gracious heart; I am grateful for my career; I am grateful for my colleagues; I am grateful to be volunteering; I will be the light for someone today. I am going to have a wonderful day.

It is important to be cognizant of the fact that we are each writing our own stories, and we each have the opportunity to make ourselves the heroine or hero of it.

And so, love yourself unconditionally; speak well of yourself. Believe in yourself; love those around you; be grateful to those who have helped along the way and eased your path. Forgive yourself and others; both kinds of forgiveness need to be unconditional to really work.

I have repeated the following affirmations a few times in the course of this book because I have seen how powerful they can be and how they can open our hearts. Affirm to yourself:

I am too positive to be doubtful; I am too optimistic to be fearful; I am too determined to be defeated; I am the light within. The light does not discriminate; it shines on us all if we are open to receiving it.

When we don't believe in our authentic ourselves and live according to other people's standards out of the fear-based notion that people won't like the "real" us, we dishonour and disrespect the light of our authentic selves. When we give away our power to others and live in fear, we become a mere shadow in someone else's light.

The light of our authentic selves warms our hearts and brightens our souls; it energizes our bodies and inspires our minds. This light is within each one of us. We all have the ability to shine bright, so why do we not allow ourselves to do so?

I believe one of the reasons is that many of us are afraid of change. That the bright light of our more authentic selves will intimidate others and create criticism and rejection. As such, it feels safer to stay stuck, to live in the darkness. Sadly, we are often afraid of our own light, afraid of its power and what it can do to empower us. And so we turn to negativity and begin to count other people's blessings and compare ourselves to others, wondering why they appear to be living a better life than we are. So, how do we turn this situation around? Well, again, we must first learn to love ourselves unconditionally, accept our strengths and not focus on perceived defects. We must explore opportunities to grow, to become the most authentic versions of ourselves that we can be. Remember that even diamonds have their flaws but are still sought after for their beauty and brilliance. What we feel, we attract. What we imagine, we create.

When we have faith in ourselves and stand with our heads held high, we are unstoppable.

The courage to accept people, places and circumstances that are out of our control means accepting ourselves as we are and accepting what we cannot change. Believing in ourselves also allows us to accept our defects of character that need changing, and then doing so with love and a lighter heart. Change and self-transformation are parts of life, an opportunity that must be embraced without fear in order to evolve, grow and attain our soul purpose in life.

And so I ask you as you read this chapter to take a moment to smile, both outwardly and inwardly, because today you are stronger than you were yesterday, and tomorrow you will be even stronger still. With strength comes courage, and with courage comes will.

"Never apologize for who you are. It lets the whole world down," as Jen Sincero says in *You Are a Badass: How to Stop Doubting Your Greatness and Start Living an Awesome Life* (Running Press Adult, 2020). You are perfect just as you are. Should you be less quirky, curvier, more or less outspoken, more or less anything? Says who? "Your job is to be as you as you can be," says Sincero, the only "you" the world will ever see, so it's a mistake to deny the world its one and only chance to experience and benefit from your unique qualities.

At the end of the day, what could be more important than honouring ourselves by investing 100 per cent of our very beings into believing in ourselves and our singular soul purpose in life — the reason that we are here on this Earth?

What better way to honour the Universe than by being our most authentic selves, the absolute best version of who we were put on this Earth to be.

Be daring.
Be different.
Be you.
Be light.
Be love.

I find that when I practise the rituals that I have laid out in this chapter and am dedicated to fulfilling my authentic soul purpose, one that is dusted with laughter, love and service, I am successful in rewriting any outsider story that tries to make me feel less than, or not quite "enough" or not worthy of the love that comes from beginning and renewing friendships and loving partner relationships.

I am empowered to pen my own life story, chapter by chapter, line by line because, when I honour myself, when I honestly and authentically believe in myself and my personal life's purpose, I become the very best and most authentic version of myself.

And because life is known to interrupt our lives with both big and little missteps along the way, that little gap when our guard might slip just a little and self-doubt does its best to creep in, it is important to remember to be kind to ourselves, that if we fall back into old behaviours at any point in our day or week to not stress about it. When we've done the work involved to be our most authentic selves — and actualize being "the more" of who we want to be, we can always begin where we are and grow constantly forward along the continued path of our soul purpose. As Ruth Bader Ginsburg, the late beloved associate justice of the United States Supreme Court, once said, "I would like to be remembered as someone who used whatever talent she had to do her work to the very best of her ability."

The opportunity is available to us all when we commit to doing the work to actualize our own self-worth on the road to a brilliantly actualized soul purpose. Truly believing in ourselves is our heart's light, and when we become our own cheerleaders, unequivocally believing in our soul purpose and self-worth in this life, we become the light that guides us forward toward purposeful principles and ethics.

The honest work of believing in myself and greeting each day with joy and a strong sense of humour — embracing the conscious act of being true and committed to the everyday practices and habits that serve me well and actualize my soul purpose in my everyday life — is, for me, akin to the spiritual act of pumping iron to build my inner strength and spirit.

Finally, I urge you to keep close to your heart this quote from Paulo Coelho, which summarizes our intention of believing in ourselves with love, honour and respect: "In love, no one can harm anyone else; we are each responsible for our own feelings and cannot blame someone else for what we feel."

CHAPTER 6

ACTUALIZING OUR DREAMS: THEY ARE THE ENGINES OF OUR SOUL PURPOSE

"We each have our own personal destinies. Speak them; will them; action them into existence."

— Reetu Gupta

The path to living our dreams starts the very second we wake up in the morning; their origins are rooted in how we greet the day which, in turn, breathes life into our hopes and aspirations. When I tell the Universe I am looking forward to this day, that I am prepared and unstoppable, that I am committed to using my day as the next step on the road to actualizing my dreams, any fears and doubts that may try to negate my warrior dreams become whispers in the wind.

So just how did I get to this place of self-assurance — one that is driven not by ego but rather by a spiritual foundation that is rooted in self-worth and self-belief — and is empowered by my most authentic and unshakeable faith in my soul purpose?

The series of mindful-action steps that I have put into place to help me along in my journey are both strategic and spiritual. They do, however, require a sincere commitment to the process, one that I assure you is well worth the investment. As inspiration, and in order to nurture and encourage the identification and actualization of your dreams as well as your divine intentions, know that all of the chapters in this book are an accumulation of steps toward becoming our most authentic selves. When we hold a sincere and unwavering belief in our singular soul purpose, any fears that we have are no longer able to ride shotgun on our journey through life.

Identifying my dreams and being clear about how I am going to go about achieving them has taught me to be specific about what it is I want and to map out a clear path to get there, which is not to say that the dreams we initially desire cannot have some flexibility to them.

Only one thing makes our dreams impossible to achieve — and that is our fear of failing to achieve them.

Interesting.

How could the thought of making a cherished dream become a reality possibly also hold such anxiety and fear within itself?

Dreaming of the optimal career or vibrant lifestyle or loving relationship we deeply desire should be the very wish that one would want to manifest. So, what is it exactly that we fear about actualizing it?

Well, to begin with, the fear of taking those first steps and getting out of our comfort zone is rooted in a lack of believing in ourselves. It is a fact that fear and doubt kill more dreams than failure ever will.

Plus, human emotions are both complex and complicated. Some of us might believe — actually fear — that we are not worthy, that we don't deserve to be the equivalent of a light-filled, love-centred dream-catcher. Piled on top of that is fear of not being able to achieve the goals we have set for ourselves, which of course then wraps itself around the fear of being judged by our peers as failures. There is fear of taking those first steps and fear of getting out of our familiar comfort zone. However, when our dreams are born from within our spiritual soul purpose and held close as sacred truths in our hearts, then the love and purpose that comes as a result ensures that our dreams will be fulfilled. So how do we go about tackling and assuaging our fears, harnessing them so that they are no longer the masters of our thoughts and actions?

Fear is an amazingly powerful emotion, one that can be either a natural phenomenon or one that contagiously embeds itself into our very beings through its negative transmission by others who do not want to see us succeed and thrive. In fact, as mentioned previously, I feel so strongly about the impact that fear can have on a person's life that I have changed, as you now know, acronym FEAR from Fear Everything and Run to Face Everything and Rise. I manifest this saying with what is now a familiar affirmation to you:

I am.
I can.
I will.

The words, the very narratives that we speak to ourselves, have the power to create our personal destinies. They are the prevailing engines that have the wherewithal to transform both our own lives and those around us.

And so if someone tries to tell us, "You cannot; you are not; you will not," then it is up to each one of us to chase off that voice and write that voice right out of our very psyche. It is also critically important to keep in mind that we are all gifted with both strengths and weaknesses. When we believe in ourselves we are doing just that — believing and having faith in our own abilities.

The choice to listen to the inner voice that affirms and supports the truths of our dreams — that they are valid, reasonable and doable — is up to each one of us. When we make that decision, we defuse the voice of the mocking saboteur who tells us that we cannot, should not or will not. And really, why should any of us ever give credence or power to someone who deems our efforts as failures? It is critically important to remember that we are the creators and owners of our personal destinies; we need to allow the voice of our intuition and personal hearts to guide us in our dream manifestations.

Intriguingly, when our body sends us messages demanding that we look after our hunger, thirst or pain, we are quick to comply. But when our heart speaks, too often we drown out its intuitive voice in favour of the white noise surrounding us or the critical voices and opinions of others who jealously speak their discontent.

As soul-purpose warriors however, we need to be accountable to live our best lives and to follow our heart's desires. Who better to honour our life intentions than the self-directed spirit that resides inside of our minds, bodies and souls?

"Dream is not the thing you see in sleep but it is the thing that doesn't let you sleep," said A.P.J. Abdul Kalam, who was India's president from 2002 to 2007. His words have had a profound effect on me because I have always felt similarly — that there are dreams we have when we sleep, and then there are those dreams that we cannot let sleep. Allow yourself to dream and then make those dreams your goals. Live your dreams.

I dream my dreams.
I envision the possibilities.
I believe that the dreams in my heart are waiting for me to achieve them.
I am capable of achieving my dreams.
I can make my dreams come true.
I will make my dreams come true.

We all go through difficult times; no one goes untouched.

In fact, at times, it almost feels like we are being tested by the all-encompassing Universe. As I have stated previously, I vehemently do not believe, however, that God is ever testing us. Rather, I believe that He puts challenges in front of us that He knows we can handle and can conquer. He gives us the free will and the power to believe in ourselves as a means to honouring ourselves and our life's purpose. Rather than a test, I believe it is a testament to God's love and belief in us that we can successfully handle the challenges that life presents, which, in turn, makes the actualization of our dreams that much more poignant.

As a part of manifesting and actualizing my dreams, I have learned that I must be willing: willing to grow, willing to accept change, willing to embrace transformation, and willing to be open to the Universe's messages. For when we allow this transformation to happen, our perspective shifts, and we are able to allow love, light, magic and joy into our lives. The Universe responds in kind by lighting the path that transports us to the central core of our dreams.

A real-life example of the powers of transformation can be witnessed by the journey that a caterpillar takes. In order to actualize its soul purpose — that is, to become a butterfly — a caterpillar must first enter into a dark chrysalis and stay there from anywhere between five and 21 days before it emerges as an enchanting and colourful butterfly. And while the life cycle of a butterfly such as that of the Monarch is extremely short — two to six weeks — the gifts that these beloved insects bestow on nature as they carry pollen which in turn nurtures fruits, vegetables and plants to produce seeds, cannot be overestimated. In fact, in Native American culture, butterflies represent transformation, comfort, hope and positivity.

Similarly, each one of us has the power to pollinate our own dreams by bestowing the positive effects of light, laughter and hope on those we come in contact with on a daily basis. If you are having trouble imagining and envisioning yourself actualizing your dreams, adopt the butterfly as your symbol of change; your personal metamorphosis will allow you to live life authenticating your most passionate dreams.

A warrior mind refuses to give in or give up and does not accept no for an answer — to me, "no" just means that I need to seek out new options and do more research and fact-finding to actualize what it is I am trying to achieve. Personally, the only way I know that I have given up too early is if I haven't achieved the dream I was going for.

At the end of the day, if every reasonable and honest effort has been made and for whatever reason your dream is not something that is realistically going to happen, I recommend taking a step back to assess what you could have or might have done better in your pursuit of that particular goal. If I've put my best foot forward and have given it my all-out best effort, then I look to see what the lesson is and then regroup from there.

Let me share an example with you about how I took a dream I was passionate about and genuinely wanted to actualize but eventually had to accept that it was a dream that needed to evolve into one that was a better fit for my integrity and lifestyle.

Having a deep-rooted love for fashion, my first inclination was to be a model, as I mentioned previously. I went on many commercial modelling interviews and tryouts where I was routinely told I looked "too Indian," or "not Indian enough," or that my size or my hair wasn't right — the negative feedback was endless. After many such interactions, I realized that modelling did not align with my values and how I wanted to be treated or how it made me feel inside, and so I did some honest soul-searching about what my dream really looked like and what I wanted to get from it. After listening to my heart, which I consider the engine of my soul purpose, I realized that I would be intuitively serving my soul purpose designing fashions rather than modelling them. And so I went for it, aligning my clothing lines with my values of inclusivity, acceptance and change, and created a showcase collection of women's fashions and then put on a one-day show, effectively actualizing a 2.0 reiteration of my fashion dreams. From this experience I learned to be willing and more open to morphing my dreams into even better and greater versions of themselves.

I would like to share a couple of other examples of dream-catchers who I am confident you can identify with; ordinary people with everyday challenges and obstacles who went after their hearts' desires to actualize the kinds of dreams that have made an enduring impact, not just within their own circles but also as strong influencers among the broader public.

Almost everyone is familiar with the name Maya Angelou, the beloved poet and civil rights activist.

After being sexually assaulted as a young child, Angelou became mute and did not speak for five years, and after her uncle went on to kill her attacker, the trauma in her young life was only increased, a series of events that she wrote about in her autobiography, *I Know Why the Caged Bird Sings* (1969). Not only did Angelou overcome these incredibly distressing events to find her voice as the author of several books of poetry, seven autobiographies and three books of essays, she also became a champion and advocate for race equality, helping raise funds to support Dr. Martin Luther King Jr.'s Southern Christian Leadership Conference.

Actualizing one of her famous quotes, "Dare to let your dreams reach beyond you," Angelou did just that. Knowing that her dreams were tied to infinite possibilities, she became a leading dream-catcher, whose efforts have impacted generations.

Another dream-maker that you are well familiar with by now is Paulo Coelho, who while enjoying success in the career he'd been pursuing, still felt that he was not realizing the dream that was closest to his heart. In 1986, Coelho had a spiritual awakening as he walked the 500-plus mile Santiago de Compostela trail, one that was a turning point in his life. He realized that although he was very happy — he had a person he loved, he enjoyed the work he was doing and it earned him a living — he was not fulfilling his dream, which was to be a writer. That deep desire to fulfil his dream to be a writer has been a gift to us all. Since it was first published in 1988 in Portuguese, *The Alchemist* has sold tens of millions of copies and has been translated into 56 languages. In fact, it holds the Guinness World Record as the most translated book by a living author.

Our dreams can and do have the great possibility of becoming realities if and when we allow ourselves to believe and have faith in the process — and in ourselves.

Do you ever wonder what happened to the magical wonderment we had when we were children? Our imaginations were enchanting and our curiosity was so strong that the dreams that we dreamed — anything from being a firefighter to a ballerina — was exactly who we saw ourselves being. Unfortunately, when we became adults many of us lost this sense of wonderment and the simple belief that life is dusted with the magic of becoming.

As children, we believe that anything is possible, the world is our playground. But as we get older, society teaches us that there are responsibilities and accountabilities, boundaries and parameters that must be adhered to. It deems that certain careers or societal roles are skewed toward masculine energy or skills. (Although, thankfully, society is slowly but surely changing some of these perceptions, albeit not fast enough.) It is the kind of feedback that I have been given many times on my journey.

And so, our sense of wonderment and curiosity diminishes as we get older because these limiting societal norms drive many of us to capitulate to them if we want to be accepted "into the fold." But as we have learned throughout the pages of this book, when we embrace an unflagging affirmative belief in ourselves we empower our ability to stand up for what we want in order to maximize the very essence of our dreams.

Dr. Martin Luther King Jr. said it best: "You don't have to see the whole staircase, just take the first step."

Of course, in order to actualize our dreams, we have to know the details, the specifics of what they look like, which is ultimately the difference between daydreaming and dreams. As a part of my dream planning, at the beginning of each year I take some time to sit in silence, set my intentions (while, of course, also doing some daydreaming, among my favourite things to do). I then put pen to paper and spend a couple of hours writing down my most important and self-affirming dream intentions, ones that I intend to accomplish in that year. I trust my heart, my instinct and my intuition to guide me as I pour my intentions into what I call my Magic Journal. In the process of writing these dreams down, my mind sees what my heart intends to actualize, and those very intentions then become both a conscious and subconscious part of my psyche. Once I have written down my goals for the year, which I have taken quality time to envision, I place my journal in my sacred place, where it stays until the year is over. The importance of this exercise is such that when I do go back to my Magic journal at the end of each year, most, if not all, of the dreams that I have written down have been actualized.

If you were told your dreams have infinite possibilities, what would that look like to you?

I encourage you to pause here for a few moments to pick up a pen, open your journal, or a notepad, or even a note on your phone and spend five to seven minutes writing free-flow ideas about your dreams and how you envision yourself achieving them. I promise you that you will discover that there is a magic to writing your dreams down, even the most whimsical, fantastical ones. Write them down. Believe in them. And then send them into the Universe.

As you have read many times in this book, the Universe will conspire with us to help us achieve our dreams, but it is up to us to do the work of being clear and honest with ourselves about what we want to actualize.

Affirmation:
I am here.
I am happy.
I am inspired.
I am, I can and I will actualize and honour my dreams.

Positive self-talk can and does go a long way to actualizing our dreams. I find that the words I speak to myself, when they come from a loving, kind place of confidence and belief in myself, empower me on my path forward. I breathe these thoughts out and exhale them into the Universe with great faith and intent. And I do the work, on a daily basis if possible, or at least three to five times a week. Meditating, sitting in silence, and writing my dreams down empowers my mind with clarity and focus so that it knows what my heart desires.

In order to keep my dreams alive and spark their living intentions in every aspect of my life, I include this tagline in all my email signatures: "For the love of pursuing passions," which to me is a statement of continuous and committed manifestation that informs the Universe that I am taking the steps every day to make my dreams a reality.

Of course, no matter what our age, in order to be self-actualized we must take the time to take a step back and say, "Who do I want to be, what do I want out of life and how can I contribute to the well-being of those around me?"

Personally, I prioritize the time to daydream, for what better way to spend a few moments in our rush-about lives than to take the time to dream, to be curious and to look at things around us with a sense of wonderment and delight? Having a passion for something that is of interest is the key that unlocks the door to the affirming feelings of expectation, joy and awe, everyday gifts like the beauty found in a wildflower growing at the side of the road or the smile of a baby who just smiles for the sake of doing so. In fact, even in the everyday experiences of life, extraordinary moments can happen, like connecting with other fans as you cheer your home team on to victory, or giving or receiving unexpected kindnesses, or being open to unplanned adventures. There are so many life moments to be grateful for. And just why are these little snapshots in life so important? Because they open up the window to life's possibilities around what is and what can be, and they gift us with a light heart, a general sense of well-being and the opportunity to dream our best dreams.

In order to not become overwhelmed, know that it is perfectly OK to begin where you are — six months from now, you will celebrate those first steps that you decide to take today. Saying "Now is not the time" is neither a valid reason nor an acceptable excuse. God made us exactly who we are for a reason; the Universe needs each of our singular talents, character traits and passions in order to make this world a better place to be. We may look at ourselves and see character defects and weaknesses, but we were created exactly for those reasons. When we tell ourselves we are here for a reason, for our own specific soul purpose, we are honouring the Universe's intentions.

A powerful belief in what we can manifest and what we can achieve is nurtured and cultivated by these two simple words: I am. In fact, when we wrap our intentions and dreams in the powerful affirmation that is "I am" — "I am powerful, I am creative, I am going to achieve my dreams, I achieve my dreams" — we become our own dream manifestors.

As well, it is important to always have faith in the process. Difficult times come with their own poignant lessons; they strengthen us, gift us with new skills and the opportunity and great heart to look at situations with a new lens and perspective — all of which prepare us with the tools to fulfil our own destinies.

And when you are going through difficult times on the way to fulfilling your dreams, try saying this affirmation:

I am too positive to be doubtful.

I am too optimistic to be fearful.
I am too determined to be defeated.

Another mindset that has served me well is embodied in the spirit of openness and willingness to consider and allow my dreams to morph and evolve into new, bigger or different possibilities. Plus, it is important to own our dreams — to count on ourselves and our inner soul purpose — to actualize our dreams. I tend to keep my dreams close to my heart, trusting only a very few close confidants, most especially my brother, Suraj, to walk my walk of dreams with me, cherished friends and family members whose sole soul purpose is to lift me up rather than tear me down along my journey, supporting my belief that the word "impossible" is really only a two-word mission statement of affirmation: "I'm possible."

When I give voice to my heart and listen for the Universe's direction with patience, love and wonder, I have found that the answer always presents itself. While it might not always be the one that I am looking for or possibly hoping for, most often it is the answer that best serves me in the pursuit of my dreams.

Change is life's responsibility and transformation is ours. Life doesn't get better by chance; it gets better when we are willing and open to the possibilities inherent in change. As the Chinese military strategist and philosopher Sun Tzu wrote more than two millennia ago in his book, *The Art of War*, "Let your plans be dark and impenetrable as night, and when you move, fall like a thunderbolt."

In other words, when I go about pursuing my dreams with focused intent, determination and strength, I am equipped with the power to ensure the successful actualization of them. It is a philosophy that I live by in the quest for my dreams. Listening to my intuition, a voice that has only gotten stronger as I do the work with a grateful heart, allows me to trust that even in the darkest and most challenging times, all is well even when it doesn't feel like it. Successful people focus on the positives, the "what is" rather than the "don't haves." They focus on what they excel at rather than weakening their intent with the things that they may have no talent for. They focus instead on the possibilities.

An important aspect in the journey of dreams, and really in most aspects of our lives, is to gift ourselves with little rewards that are relevant to our achievements thus far.

As Nelson Mandela advised, "Remember to celebrate milestones as you prepare for the road ahead."

Whether it is the gift of a day off, lunch with friends after many days of hard work, a fine bottle of wine, or even a sparkling new journal, acknowledging our efforts is a motivator and an affirmation of encouragement to keep going.

When we do the work of setting our Divine intentions, our spirit then becomes the enabling force behind the actualization of our dreams.

And so when your inner voice whispers to you: "What if I fail?" take it gently by the hand and say, "But what if I fly?" As former First Lady Eleanor Roosevelt once said, "The future belongs to those who believe in the beauty of their dreams." And so, you may ask, "How have I best actualized my dreams?"

Well, I have worked with sincere determination and an honest heart, and I have found that my dreams have then been able to manifest in ways that I previously never imagined possible.

Believe. Just believe and do the work I have suggested within these pages and I guarantee that your dreams will be manifested and actualized in ways that you could only previously have dreamed about.

What will you weave into your dreamcatcher today, this week or this year?

CHAPTER 7

EMBRACING AND BLESSING THE STRUGGLES: OVERCOME FEAR TO ACCEPT CHANGE AND EFFECT TRANSFORMATION

"The period of greatest gain in knowledge and experience is the most difficult period in one's life."

— Dalai Lama

What doesn't kill you makes you stronger.

How many times has someone said this to you as you find yourself going through a tumultuous, challenging and painful event, a time in your life when you are not able to fathom just how you will ever come out the other side with any kind of strength or hope left intact?

Human nature is such that we tend to be our best selves when everything is going our way. But life does not happen in a bubble — each one of us is presented with our own series of challenges and struggles — no one goes untouched. The good news is, however, that if we do the work, if we are mindfully dedicated to actualizing the tenets outlined in the earlier chapters of this book — which include living life with courage and conviction, a loving heart, affirmative habits and small daily acts of gratitude — we can and will come to a spirit place that embraces the struggles rather than cursing and bemoaning them. Sounds unbelievable ... unrealistic, even?

I am here to tell you that it is possible, that when I honestly adopt a spirit of willingness to change my perspective and open my heart to the lessons that are wrapped like precious nuggets of gold within the challenges in my life, I come to a place that allows me to embrace and then bless the struggles that are presented to me within every aspect of my life.

Examining the ways in which we are able to embrace life's struggles is the first step on the path to doing so. Integral to this is the honesty and willingness to be accountable for whatever part we might have played in a relationship or event that has imploded on us and caused us to be embroiled in the hardships at hand.

We recognize that our life's trials come in many forms and on many platforms, possibly leaving us financially challenged or spiritually bankrupt. But how we present ourselves during these times should be in line with our authentic selves so that we can come to a place of fulfilment and gratitude. It is the energy we bring to the tests we are faced with and the ultimate willingness to embrace a shift in perspective that play a key role in our ability to handle our struggles with grace and positivity. This means we need to surrender the outcome of whatever issue we are going through and place it in the Universe's hands. No matter how much is lost, there is always goodness and value that is present and ready to be created.

No matter what we have done or what has happened, if we honestly commit to doing the "do" things, which include embracing the change that is needed, we will then have the ability to affect what can be.

A powerful and dynamic approach to blessing our struggles is to take some quiet time, a few brief moments to say the affirmation below, which will help connect the inner spirit to the Universe, which in turn will guide us toward our heart's soul purpose:

I have the strength to accept the things I cannot change.
I have the insight to change the things that I can.
I have the wisdom to know the difference.
And I have the courage to walk away from the people, places and things that no longer serve me.

It is also highly critical to understand the importance of surrendering the outcome of our challenges to the Universe, to a Higher Power or to a God of our understanding. We need to realize that when we surrender the outcome to the Universe, it does not mean that we are giving up. Rather, we are putting forward our very best efforts and, from that point on, we are allowing the outcome to be one that best serves our life's intentions and our authentic soul purpose. For when the Universe asks us to put our faith in the powers that be, what we are actually being asked to do is open our hearts so that by the act of surrendering, we are giving the Divine Universe permission to release us from our pain and suffering. We are not told to surrender five per cent of our struggles, rather we are instructed to surrender all of our problems.

To surrender means to walk our path with confidence and courage, knowing that a greater force is with us. As in the Bhagavad Gita, when Arjun was preparing to go into battle, he had to walk the path, fight the battle and then surrender the outcome to Krishna. Similarly, we too must surrender the outcome once we can truly and confidently say that we have done everything in our power that we could possibly do to find solutions to the challenges we are experiencing. From that point forward, we need to allow the Universe to step in and provide us with our best outcome.

When we use what we learned in Chapter 5 about believing in ourselves, we intuitively know that our faith in ourselves, which is rooted in the three Cs of courage, conviction and confidence, will shepherd us through the pain to the solution. We will then come to a point where we will be able to bless our struggles, accepting that they are ultimately gifts in disguise, which in turn allows us to grow into stronger and more authentic, auspicious versions of ourselves. However difficult it may seem, there is always a path, always a solution to overcoming our challenges, ones that are guided by our intuitive hearts, our determination and our courage. As such, it is imperative to have a genuine faith in the Universe and its ability to put us in the exact situation that we need to be in in order to not only accept our struggles but also bless them with a positive and grateful heart.

So, what is it that I mean when I say we need to bless our struggles? Well, I mean we need to marshal the fortitude to look at our situation and see beyond the pain we are mired in so that we are able to truly embrace the inherent lessons that are wrapped within our struggles. We need to see and truly appreciate the divine reason that we were put in this particular situation and also remember that the Universe or the Greater Power of our choice only gives us as much as we can handle, nothing more and nothing less.

When we let go of fear, we have the power and strength to move forward and face the situation or circumstance that presents itself. Once we do that, we can accept “what is” and embrace the path forward.

Negative emotions carry a heavy energy and, in fact, weigh us down. Our body language changes when we are sad, afraid or struggling with a problem. For example, we will often show our distress by drawing our arms into our body, our shoulders will be slouched, and we tend not to look a person in the eye, all of which are symptoms of stress and anxiety. Once these negative emotions are released, however, we are lighter, and our body expands as if to take in more energy.

It is so important to remember that change is life’s responsibility but, at the same time, we are accountable for our own personal transformation. We must choose to use our life struggles to transform ourselves. A good example of this can be seen in nature, where transformation takes place on a daily basis. This is the Universe's way of gently reminding us about the beauty of the process. A caterpillar is cocooned for about two weeks in complete isolation and darkness. But the caterpillar does not give up. She rather keeps her faith in the process of transformation, using her own energy to metamorphose. Once the transformation is complete, the final result is one that emerges in a burst of colours and wings, which then takes the once lowly caterpillar to new heights — a lofty kingdom it had never dared to previously imagine.

Change, if we allow it to, gives us the wings and the freedom to pursue possibilities that we might not have otherwise imagined. And so, it is essential to allow change to be a welcome part of who we are, allowing it to flow through us as it defines and nurtures our spiritual path forward.

The Dalai Lama explains that when we face our suffering we are able to also face our problems and solve them. He says, "If you directly confront your suffering, you will be in a better position to appreciate the depth and nature of the problem."

Our past choices, actions and decisions have led us to this present moment and have been the contributing factors to who we are today — often in positive and self-affirming ways. But, for many of us, the past represents times of regret, self-recrimination, pain and negative experiences. It is not only important, but life-definingly vital, to realize that no matter how much we may want to, we cannot change what happened in our pasts. What we can do, however, is take the knowledge from past transgressions and past regrets and embrace them as lessons. Rather than being full of misgivings, shame and the subsequent self-criticism and spirit-bashing, we can make the decision to be better human beings, ones who are thoughtful, kind and loving. Knowledge is power — the power to change who we want to be today and who we aspire to be tomorrow. Today's decisions impact tomorrow's truths.

When new opportunities, new relationships, new ideas or ways of doing things come along, I welcome them with open arms and an open heart. I find a beauty and magic to life's mysteries, and I choose to view these opportunities as blessings. Some people believe in luck, but I believe in destiny. I believe there comes a time when opportunity meets preparedness, and the Universe presents us with this new life experience because as a Divine Being with faith, the certainty is that we are ready to receive and embrace this new freedom.

Our souls are connected to the Divine Universe, and when we are open to receiving the messages it reveals to us, we will be transformed. Our mind will shift from what was to what can be, an evolution of grace, hope and positivity that will light and actualize the path forward to our Divine Feminine purpose.

It is a state of being that assures us that all is well even as we sit in the midst of chaos. Our resolve and knowledge is strengthened by knowing that our loving hearts continue to make the life-altering difference.

I would like to share with you a favourite example of what strength and power looks like to me as symbolized by the great and mighty tiger, an animal which, in many cultures, symbolizes illumination, energy and protection.

I like to imagine that a tiger's black and orange stripes represent the balance of yin and yang energy, the equivalent of light and dark and the virtues of strength, victory and virtue. And because a tiger symbolizes these qualities, there are hunters and elements of nature who want to fight this majestic breed. But adult tigers tend not to fear their predators in the wild — elephants, hyenas and mankind — because tigers have faith in their own strength and never doubt their prowess and power to defend and protect what is theirs.

The tiger is my symbol, my inner narrative that whispers to me that no challenge or upset has the ability to change who I am;

my authentic self is not compromised by the dark spaces that I have to negotiate my way through. I am strength; I am virtue; I am victory.

In fact, we all have the ability to be tigers, an image that is key to remember when the swirl of life presents difficulties. We have all had experiences when things aren't going our way and we start saying things such as "Why me? Why did that happen? Why now?" But when we do this, we forget to count our own blessings because we are too busy counting someone else's. But when we shift our perspective and honestly look at each challenge, struggle or loss that *we* go through, we will see that we have learned a host of valuable lessons. When we let go of our pasts, open our minds and our hearts to change, try our best and then surrender the outcome, our faith and trust in the Universe's love and positive intentions will manifest the best possible outcome for us.

It is about dispelling doubt and replacing it with courage, confidence and a belief in self.

When Muhammad Ali was fighting his way to the top — literally — he told himself every day, "I am the greatest," even before he knew he was. Rather than doubting himself and being overwhelmed with the obstacles he faced, he kept his vision close to his heart, and he embraced and accepted every challenge with determination, stamina and an unshakeable faith in himself.

And that is where the importance of faith comes in — having faith that we are exactly where we are meant to be, having faith in our abilities, in the Divine Universe and in the God of our understanding.

I would like to share with you an example of how facing a struggle head-on with courage, resilience and conviction came to impact not only the person involved but also the very fabric of society.

Viola Desmond, an African-Canadian, was born on July 6, 1914 in Halifax, Nova Scotia. A businesswoman and civil libertarian,

Viola was a mentor to young Black women who attended her Desmond School of Beauty Culture. In 1946, at the age of 32, Viola attended a movie at New Glasgow's Roseland Theatre, where she refused to move from her seat in the "whites only" section. Although she was told that she could purchase only a balcony seat, Viola took a seat at the front anyway, at which time she was forcibly removed, arrested, held in jail overnight, and then charged, tried and convicted of tax evasion. That charge, based on the one cent difference in tax between floor and balcony seats, was the only possible legal justification for her arrest and imprisonment. The physical injury, humiliation and injustice that Desmond suffered outraged the African-Canadian community in Nova Scotia. The case became a rallying point for those seeking to end discrimination in their province, including the newly established Nova Scotia Association for the Advancement of Coloured People, which unsuccessfully contested her conviction. Despite the outcome of her legal case, Viola Desmond's act of resistance has come to represent a turning point in the struggle for rights in Canada. In 2010, the Government of Nova Scotia issued an apology and a posthumous pardon, and, in 2016, the federal government announced that Desmond would be commemorated on the newly designed $10 bill.[1]

To me, Viola's confidence and her ability to rise above what was a highly charged and disturbing situation, one that was unequivocally due to the colour of her skin, defines the very act of blessing the struggle. To conduct herself with the grace and courage of her convictions in the midst of what for many at the time would have been overwhelming is, for me, the secret of life. Rising above the criticisms and negative remarks of others as I face the challenges in my life the best way I know how, allows me to both bless my own struggles and be a conduit to passing those blessings on to others in my life.

Another example that I would like to share with you that is

1. https://parks.canada.ca/culture/designation/personnage-person/viola-desmond

closer to home for me happened in the fall of 2019, when the Toronto Raptors were in the NBA championship race for the Larry O'Brien Trophy.

The Toronto Raptors — which I know you are quite familiar with by now — were playing the two-time defending champions, the Golden State Warriors. I was in attendance for Game 3 of the NBA Finals best-of-seven series, which was being played in Oakland, California and, understandably, tensions were running high. The Raptors were ahead by 10 points when their point guard, #7, Kyle Lowry, dove out of bounds to get possession of the ball and landed in a seat next to Mark Stevens, the Golden State Warriors minority owner. Mark proceeded to shove Lowry aggressively while cursing at him. As I watched this interaction, my heart sank because it was clear to me that racial discrimination was involved, that Stevens was treating Lowry in a disgusting, hateful way because of his race. Lowry, however, handled this challenging and unexpected situation with supreme class and grace, which I found poignant and inspiring. The majority of fans could see the whole confrontation on camera as Lowry was shoved, yelled at and sworn at by Stevens. Lowry, however, extricated himself from the situation while showing no visible emotional reaction to the abuse. He just looked straight at Stevens, shook his head and walked back out onto the court. In my opinion, the whole situation was disgusting — in fact, demeaning — but the way Lowry handled it showed the world that when we approach a challenge, even an unwarranted and unfair one, with love and tolerance rather than violence, we can, either individually or collectively, affect game-changing results.

Life doesn't get better by chance — it gets better by change. In fact, as I have reminded you before in the pages of this book, change is life's responsibility, while transformation is our responsibility.

Another key component that I find integral to the process of blessing the struggles and challenges in my life is the practice of active forgiveness. When my heart is troubled by something that someone has done to, for, or against me, I use this short affirmation to clear my mind and move forward with a positive spirit:

I am confident.
I am powerful.
I am strong.
I am prosperous.
All that I need to be my most authentic self blossoms within me today.

As I continue to walk the path of life seeking to actualize my most auspicious self, I consciously refuse to engage in the tit-for-tat, fighting-fire-with-fire attitude. I know that I do not need to build myself up to become bigger in others' eyes, which, as we all know, is a fool's game — a game of denial, really — for the very person we need to convince that we are strong, confident and worthy is ourselves.

As Mother Teresa said, "When we spend time judging others, we don't have time to love them."

Instead, I approach life's struggles with an attitude of gratitude and love, one that allows me to put my own integrity and self-respect first. And that takes courage. It takes courage to think before we act, reflect before we speak, and genuinely care about the person in front of us.

The more challenges we encounter in our lives, the greater the experiences are around how to build our inner strength to meet our problems with a calm heart and an appreciation for our ability to come out the other side. It is how we bolster our thinking to help us through the maze of life.

Approaching our problems in an ego state of mind, like "I don't deserve what has happened," or "Why me?" or "Why not me?" is the arrogance of denial that comes from feeling insecure or fearful. Humility is not the same thing as being timid, shy or fearful.

Fears and insecurities are a part of life's daily challenges, and how we react to these negative emotions is what separates the wheat from the chaff. Even a happy life is not without its measure of darkness. If you think about it, the word "happiness" would lose its meaning if it were not balanced by sadness. Living life *with* happiness, not *for* happiness, is a belief that I have espoused in several chapters in this book.

One of the other ways — and there are many — that I am able to manage the challenges in my life is by maintaining a calm, unflappable composure amidst the chaos and white noise. I know that if I keep my head held high and my mind quiet rather than being embroiled in the negativity of the situation or interpersonal dynamics, I am able to create solutions with poise and positivity. I am a firm believer that all struggles, although they might present as obstacles, are, in truth, poignant lessons in living life with positivity and grace. I genuinely believe that I am on this Earth for a reason and that I am responsible for using the resources that I am privileged to enjoy as a means to helping other people who are in need — whether that be at home or on a broader, global scale. I know that change is life's responsibility and that transformation is mine. What we think we become. And, I know that, rather than being fearful or weighed down by life's hardships and misfortunes, I can achieve what lies in front of me because I have done the personal work of envisioning my soul purpose. I am and will continue to be the best possible version of myself by being an open-minded and active listener to the Universe's messages and my heart-centred consciousness-based intuition.

I know that whatever I do today is a result of the honest and genuine soul-searching that I did yesterday. I subscribe to the Dalai Lama's message that when we have compassion — and allow that to be our motivation — we will have no regrets in life.

It is a significant teaching because, more often than not, we have no idea of what other people are going through on a daily basis. That person that cut us off at the intersection might very well have a sick child or parent at home that they are rushing to get to. That acquaintance at the coffee shop who did not acknowledge us, or that person who was short with us at work, might be deeply engaged in a struggle of their own and completely unaware of our presence.

When we gather our blessings each morning before we leave the house and then gift them to the people we meet throughout our day — most especially the ones who are unkind or difficult with us — it transforms both how we feel within ourselves as well as the person to whom we have shared our gift of a blessing. Like a yawn or a smile, the blessing of kindness and genuine caring is contagious; it is an act of pure gratitude that allows us to be conduits for God's blessings and goodwill.

I have a metaphorical magic box that symbolizes the Universe that I would like to share with you. Inside of it are the seeds of love, faith and courage that I've planted and have continually flourished because of the love, faith and courage that I put into it. Not so unexpectedly, it is these joyful qualities that are reciprocated back to me. There is no mystery in the fact that when I put unconditional love and happiness into this magic box of mine, I receive these things back. However, when I am not mindful or if I have a gap — when I haven't done the work to light this box in an affirming way, or if I input small rocks of stress, anger and jealousy — that is what the box will release back into the Universe through me.

If I plant one seed, I will receive one flower.
If I plant a handful of seeds, I will get a garden.
A seed changes into a sprout, a sprout into a flower.

There are many things we can change in life as we bloom where we're planted, but the past is not one of those things. We also need to be mindful of the person who looks at our garden and tells us how we should take care of it; they are not true gardeners, but merely people who want to contain our plentiful harvest.

The act of staying positive, accepting that hardships shape who we are, and knowing that when the fear of fighting for what we want is a tool on the way to helping us accept change, then we are on our way to actualizing positive solutions to our challenges. Transformation cannot happen without change. We have all heard the saying that we don't know how strong we are until being strong is the only choice we have. And when we change how we think about ourselves, we can change the trying and challenging situations in front of us. A diamond cannot be polished without friction, and gold cannot be purified without fire. The goodness of what can be is far more powerful than any memory of what has been. So, I encourage you as you read this to let yourself embrace this concept fully. Take the best of what you can imagine and live it with all your heart, with all that you have.

A beautifully effective way to accept change is to remain positive, saying daily expressions of gratitude for what we have, what we have been blessed with. Simple tasks and enjoyments in life, such as being able to read, being present in this day, in this life, in this bountiful country are wonderful examples. Positive thoughts lead to elevated thinking. When we are elevated we are lighter, and negative vibrational energies cannot affect us.

Indeed, a positive mind is so powerful that it has the ability to change fate and change outcomes.

A poignant example of positivity in practice is the visible manifestation that Nick Nurse, the former Toronto Raptors coach, implemented at the beginning of the 2018–2019 NBA season on the way to the team's 2019 NBA Championship win.

Nurse gave each of his coaching staff a bracelet that read "Expect To Win" at the beginning of the season. He also got bracelets made up with the initialism "AMJ," signifying April,

May, June, the NBA's basketball playoff months. Nurse's action was both a physical and symbolic message to the coaches, players and fans, as well as to all the other squads in both the Eastern and Western Conferences — that the Toronto Raptors were "in it to win it," which is exactly what the team did.

While there were, of course, a myriad of other factors involved, there is absolutely no denying the fact that the groundswell of positivity that Nick Nurse embedded in the locker room was a reason that they won the Larry O'Brien Championship Trophy.

I wear a positive attitude and embrace positive self-talk like it is a second skin to me. I tell myself multiple times throughout every day:

I am too positive to be doubtful.
I am too optimistic to be fearful.
I am too determined to be defeated.
I can achieve anything when I put my mind to it.

Buddha tells us:
You are what you think.
What you think, you become.
What you feel, you attract.

And as the 19th-century Indian Hindu monk, philosopher and religious teacher Swami Vivekananda advised in one of his inspirational teachings, "We are what our thoughts have made us; so, take care about what you think." It is a teaching that will serve us all well to hold close to our hearts. He counseled his followers to fill their minds with worthy thoughts both day and night and to aspire to the highest ideals, because "out of that will come great work," he said. The author Malcolm Gladwell once famously observed that it takes 10,000 hours of practice to master a skill, which means that we need to invest and commit to what it is we want to accomplish in life, and that includes mastering the ability to manage life's challenges with grace and a positive attitude.

Nothing is wasted along our journey; rather, as we make our way through our daily struggles with a positive mindset and a willingness to change and pivot in a direction that is affirmative to our well-being, we develop trust in ourselves as we strengthen our endurance and confidence, all in preparation for the best outcome the Universe waits to give us.

As I share with you the essence of how I manage with grace, poise and serene calmness the daily challenges that are present in my life, I would like to reiterate the importance of my daily meditation practice and the sustenance it provides, which you will read more about in Chapter 8. What is important to know in this particular context is that meditation, when practised on a consistent basis, is akin to medication for our emotional, physical and spiritual well-being. It is a proven and unequivocal fact that, when we spend quiet time in meditation and away from the chaos of the day, our stress dissipates, and when that happens our bodies release cortisol, which ultimately minimizes negativity, anxiety and worry.

Meditation allows us to conquer our fears and have faith in ourselves and in the Universe. It allows us to achieve our dreams by focusing on pathways and solutions that will help us achieve our goals.

As you read this, I would like you to take a moment to focus on your breath. As you breathe out, imagine that you are breathing out all your stress, all your worry, all your scattered thoughts.

As you breathe in, imagine yourself filling your mind, body and spirit with love, light and positivity.

Imagine living life with possibility. Imagine actualizing your dreams. Visualize attaining them.

Imagine approaching the challenges you are facing with an open heart and a desire to resolve them with compassion and empathy.

Have love for yourself.

Have love for others.

I found that when my spirit, mind and heart are quiet, my soul makes the joyful connection to the Universe, which then reveals its messages to me, providing “aha” moments of Divine inspiration and wisdom. This, in turn, illuminates my path and allows the transformation of change, growth and a new perspective to guide me through the challenges and struggles at hand. There is a beauty and magic available to each of us in life’s mysteries, and, when we make a commitment to being open to these messages, we experience the wonderfully uplifting practice of acceptance and the everlasting energy of love.

What can be begins in this moment. What can be comes from our thoughts, our actions, our commitment to positive habits and disciplines, our passion and commitment to living our best lives as we become our most auspicious, authentic selves.

The goodness of what can be is far more powerful than any memory of what has been. We need to embrace this mindset of courage, conviction, strength, love and fearlessness fully in order to turn what can be into what is. Along the way, we will learn how to open our hearts to all things that are great, all things that are positive, all things that are wrapped in love and opportunity. We will do this by focusing and renewing our energy, faith and belief in achieving anything we set our minds to.

Yesterday’s pain is today’s strength.

It isn’t about how hard things hit you, it’s about summoning the courage to get up after you’ve been hit despite your pain and keep moving forward.

One of the most valuable and joyful lessons I have learned throughout this thing called Life is that no one else can fulfil our personal soul purpose in life but ourselves — and without a shred of ego attached to this statement, but with the utmost confidence and humility, I firmly believe that no one else can be Reetu Gupta.

And just as importantly, no one else can be you.

AUSPICIOUS

We are all here for our own uniquely special purpose, and it is for that reason that we are divinely guided. Take a moment to celebrate this fact and hold it dear to your heart. And so, my fellow spiritual devotees, take the leap — imagine yourself as the hero or heroine of your own light-filled stories because heroines, in spite of their fear or doubt, soldier on.

The Universe and the Divine Feminine are waiting to welcome you as you pursue your most auspicious and authentic soul purpose.

CHAPTER 8

MEDITATION: COLLABORATING WITH THE SPIRITUAL TEACHINGS OF THE DIVINE FEMININE

"Wherever your heart is, that is where you will find your treasure."

— Paulo Coelho

Whenever I allow my heart the time and space to speak freely, I have joyfully unwrapped treasures of the heart that have filled my life with light, love and hope.

Our hearts reveal to each of us our life's intentions and our soul purpose — in truth, the very reasons why we exist. I have found that the most spiritual and heart-centring way to receive these messages of life and love is through my daily practice of meditation. The more I allow my heart to speak, the more connected I am with it and the more it shares with me. The spiritual, physical and emotional benefits of meditation are such that I actively embraced it many years ago as an integral part of my life, a spiritual force that nourishes my inner being. The practice and the benefits of meditation are such a key part of my well-being maintenance and so easily portable that no matter where I travel or how often, I always make the time to meditate and connect with the Universe by way of my heart.

In fact, meditation is such an important and effective tool in helping me live life on life's terms that I have joyfully taught the practice of meditation for over a decade now. I offer my classes for free because meditation has brought so much peace and clarity into my life — it has been a gift, really — and as such, I feel it is my duty to share these feelings of peace with others.

My older sister Reema has shared with me that my classes remind her to take the time for herself to calm and relax her mind, which she says helps her start her day with happiness and positivity.

It is a renewing experience that I wish for all of you.

And so, as we begin our journey of meditation together, I ask that you join me with an open heart so that you can readily grasp the benefits and the gifts that are a part of this wonderfully replenishing practice.

We will begin with a simple exercise that helps quiet our "monkey minds" — a Buddhist term meaning unsettled, restless, indecisive — so that you can settle in, relax and honour the teachings I am about to share with you.

Once you have found a quiet place to sit in relaxation, I will ask you to take a deep breath in, filling your chest and lungs with air. Then, exhale slowly. Inhale again, but when you exhale, this time I want you to envision that all of the worry, stress and angst that is in your mind is being released when you exhale.

Inhale one more time, and as you do so, I want you to envision that you are breathing in beautiful, loving energy as you exhale all of the unwanted negative energy that is impacting on your serenity.

In reality, the spiritual gifts of positivity, inner peace and the calmness that is serenity are the promises actualized within the consistent practice of meditation.

The beauty inherent in the process of meditation reminds me of a lotus. This flower, which starts out as a seed, buries its roots in the soil at the bottom of a water source, whether that be a pond or other watery environment. Within weeks, however, the flower sprouts as it grows toward the light, knowing that Mother Nature and the Universe will guide it as it manifests its purpose to become one of the most beautiful blossoms in nature.

Just as the lotus knows in its very essence that the warmth of the light will actualize its soul purpose on this earth, so too will we know how to guide our spirit and our heart to the divine light that is the Universe.

I am Hindu and while I have a profound connection with my religion, culture and heritage, I also have a deep love and respect for all religions. When I complete my daily meditation practice, my habit is to make the sign of a cross over my chest, a ritual that helps me feel empowered by a teaching that is in the Quran, which states "La ilaha illallah," which simply means "There is no God but God."

It is important to know and to appreciate the fact that meditation is not tied to any specific religion. In fact, prayer and meditation are, in essence, quite different. When we pray we are, in effect, having a conversation with the God or the Supreme force of our understanding, whether that be a Christian God, the Hindu Supreme Being (known as Brahma and the Holy Triad of Brahma, Vishnu and Shiva), or Yahweh, the Jewish God, Allah, the Lord of the Worlds and the Creator, in Islam. On the other hand, all that meditation requires of us is a willingness to open our minds to the possibilities available when we sit in silence and listen to our hearts. Effectively, it is the art of bringing peace and clarity to the mind through the act of stillness and quiet.

If you started down the path of a meditation practice and experienced some confusion and a feeling of not knowing how to quiet your mind and let go of the distractions in your life, you may have felt fearful or unsettled. But I am here to tell you there is nothing to be afraid of. Most people, when they think of meditation, have preconceived notions. You may have worried that it requires a level of discipline akin to that of a monk who stays in Vipassana (complete silence) for weeks at a time. Or you may worry that it requires a superhuman sense of flexibility to sit cross-legged on a hard wooden floor for unimaginable periods of time while trying desperately to purge the cascade of scattering thoughts in your overactive minds. I am here to assure you that your worries are normal and that meditation, I promise you, is accessible and achievable for any and all of us. All it takes on your part is the openness and willingness to embrace the process. It all begins with the first moment, the moment where you decide that you can and you will. That is the moment when your practice will begin to serve you.

My meditation journey began over 13 years ago when I moved into a new condo. There was a small room in my new home that was meant to be used for an office, but I had this urge to turn it into a temple and meditation room. At that point I had not welcomed meditation into my life, but a gentle voice was drawing me toward finding out more about it. Because I am a woman with deep faith, I wanted to wait until I had my temple set up to move into my new place. My mother, who is always so supportive, caring and loving, readily agreed to accompany me as I shopped for the sacred items I wanted. We came upon what appeared to be an abandoned strip mall, which had one shop that sold Indian cultural items such as small shrines and decorations. As I roamed around the dusty store, my own "monkey mind" was telling me that I would not find anything in this disheveled place. But my heart quietly told me to keep looking, and so I did because I always trust the messages I receive from my heart. And then suddenly, there it was — the perfect-size temple in pristine condition. The Universe knew what my heart's desire and passion needed in order to be actualized.

As soon as my temple was set up, my heart started speaking louder and louder to me, telling me that I should meditate. Trusting my heart, and thus allowing it to take the lead, I took a seated position, crossed my legs and closed my eyes, and I began focusing on my breath. As I breathed in and out, I could feel the energy envelop me. Visions of happiness and beautiful light presented themselves and in my mind's eye a crystal-clear image of Disney World, the happiest place on earth to me, filled my spirit with whimsical laughter. Meditation does not always have to be serious, my friends!

The first time I tried meditation I was able to focus for about 10 seconds before I started to daydream. After doing some research, I decided to use meditative music in my practice, which helped me focus on my breath. The music helped my mind to stay calm. After a period of time, however, the music became too distracting, and I felt discouraged that I was back at square one. It was at that time that I serendipitously came across a book called *An Autobiography of a Yogi*, by Paramahansa Yogananda (Self-Realization Fellowship, 1971). As I began to read this book, which described the science of meditation as well as how our bodies and souls feel at each stage of meditation, I felt similarities between Yogananda's path and my own. This encouraged me to deepen my practice by meditating in silence, which is when I felt my new habit accelerate, which, in turn, inspired me to meditate every day.

As the famous adage goes, "When the student is ready, the teacher appears" — the more I walked on this spiritual path, the more books found me and the more people would recommend certain passages or retreats to me. I was ready and so the Universe sent me multiple teachers.

A part of my daily meditation includes Pranayama.

"Prana" means energy, and "yama" means control. The practice of Pranayama is the control of our life force or breath. I started incorporating these techniques at the beginning of each meditation practice.

With these techniques I was able to meditate longer and certainly was achieving more clarity. As I continued my practice I found that, during the day, I was calmer, I could solve problems faster than others, and I just felt an overall internal sense of peace. I became so excited about these benefits that I started sharing my experiences with friends. Seeing my joy and how peaceful I had become, several of my friends asked me to teach them how to meditate so they, too, could experience what I was so obviously reaping the benefits from. I started teaching a small group of my friends, but the circle quickly grew into a large family of enthusiastic and inquisitive people, all who were eager to learn.

My own practice of silent meditation is how I start every morning. I look forward to and am grateful for the privilege of sitting in silence and allowing my heart to speak.

"It is the silence between the notes that makes the music." This is an ancient Zen observation, one that speaks to the importance of stillness and quiet during meditation practice. Silent meditation is its own form of music for the soul.

There are many benefits to meditation, the most important one today being a decreased level of stress. With the COVID-19 pandemic, the world has seen a huge increase in depression and a significant decline in mental health. When our bodies and minds experience stress, a hormone called cortisol is released, which then signals the release of other chemicals called cytokines. These chemicals causes an inflammatory response in the body, which, in turn, creates depression, increased blood pressure and anxiety. When we practice meditation and mindfulness, the levels of cortisol in our body are decreased, which helps alleviate these stress-related conditions. Post-traumatic stress disorder, fibromyalgia and irritable bowel syndrome can all be decreased as a result of consistent meditation. Decreased levels of cortisol also keeps our immune systems healthy and can ultimately prevent weight gain.

A five-year study conducted by the British Heart Foundation asked 201 patients with coronary heart disease to do Transcendental Meditation (a technique where you sit in a comfortable position with your eyes closed and silently repeat a sound, called a mantra, in your head) for 15 minutes a day.

The researchers found that this reduced the risk of death, heart attack and stroke by 48%. In addition, changes associated with lower blood pressure and lower stress levels were also noted. The researchers concluded that the practice of TM may be clinically useful in preventing further heart attacks or strokes in people who have already experienced a first such incident.

In addition to reducing stress, the study indicated that practicing a minimum of three times a week improves physical health, increases focus and concentration, enhances creativity and productivity, helps fight negativity, boosts the immune system, provides relief from chronic pain, reduces blood sugar, increases positive energy while decreasing negative energy, improves physical performance and athletic skills and improves sleep patterns.

Importantly, our meditation practices do not always have to be done in the formal way it is commonly presented. A walk in nature through a verdant forest or on a beautiful park path, one that is alive and flourishing with the replenishing gifts of nature — trees, flowers and wildlife — is a sensory and delightfully spiritual way to meditate. Watching the sun set over the ocean or hearing the crackle of a campfire on a crisp fall evening as you take in the force of the elements, all present their own meditation treasures. Really, any moment where we are silent and in tune with the Universe are acts of faith and pure gratitude, which are gifts that we receive by meditating.

And while the physical benefits of meditation are magnificent, the spiritual rewards are truly celebratory. In his book, *Buddha: A Story of Enlightenment* (HarperOne, 2009), Deepak Chopra describes Buddha's journey and the fact that most of what he learned came through meditation. How is this possible? Because when we meditate, we are connecting to the Universe, and the Universe then speaks through us and pushes life through us. Ideas will come to us and we don't know where they originated. For when we meditate, we are able to achieve self-awareness, to forgive our pasts and focus on our futures. We will find a new sense of hope, faith and happiness, which also strengthens our intuition and allows our heart to speak more clearly.

Our true sense of self, our true being, exists within each one of us. Michelangelo revealed the true form of his works hidden beneath the surface by removing material, famously stating, "The sculpture is already complete within the marble block before I start my work. It is already there. I just have to chisel away the superfluous material."

So, too, meditation removes our excess debris to reveal our true selves.

And so, herein lies the reasons that meditation practice is so important for each one of us to be aware of and integrate into our daily lives.

It is an absolute fact that every one of us has only 24 hours in our day, no matter whether we are the Pope, the president, a student, a mother, a father, a teacher or a child. We all only have the same 24 hours in our day, and it is absolutely imperative that we make the most of them. We can choose to add days to our life or we can add life to our days. It all starts from within — from our minds and our hearts.

An average human being has 70,000 thoughts running through their head on any given day. What is amazing is 95% of these thoughts are the same random thoughts from the previous day. This means that if you or I have an abundance of thoughts that are negative, anxious or stress-ridden, when we wake up the next morning we will go forward carrying around the same negative mental baggage. It is a useless cycle that creates impoverished thinking, negative attitudes and poor mental habits.

But we have a choice at any time to change this cycle. We can facilitate this by sitting in meditation and calming our monkey minds. A calm mind brings inner strength, and inner strength brings inner happiness. As a part of that, I encourage you to focus on powerful, positive thoughts, actions and attitudes, because the magic happens when we are able to do so.

If you think back to when you were a child, you might remember dressing up as a character you loved, and when you did this, the chances are you imagined yourself to be some kind of superhero, and whether you believed you were Superwoman or Superman, it is safe to say that you would have imagined it with all of your energy and might. Unfortunately, when we become adults we often lose this sense of wonder, this sense of magic, curiosity and belief in the possibilities of our dreams. But we can reignite these magical powers by focusing on what is possible ... that is the possible within the impossible.

You are in the woods and it is winter.
You have a letter, a can of beans and a magnifying glass. You do have wood. You have no match. How do you create the flame that will allow you to ignite your wood?

Well, we do this by placing the magnifying glass directly underneath the sun's rays for 50 to 60 seconds. The rays of the sun as they pass through the glass focus their heat on one specific spot, which ignites a small spark of fire.

Intriguingly, this is also how our minds work. When we focus our mind and our power on definitive meaningful goals, we have the influence to ignite the flames of our potential, which produce the results we seek.

Weak minds lead to weak results; however, strong minds have the power to perform miracles.

It is important to fill our minds with positive thoughts every day. When we say this simple mantra, *I can* and *I will*, to ourselves with great heart and intention while envisioning who we want to be, we are empowering ourselves to actualize our vision. It is then that our expectations become reality.

Even one negative thought can be toxic to our dreams; that one thought can be the stumbling block that does not allow our dreams to be realized. Usain Bolt, a multiple Olympic gold medallist and world record holder in sprinting, does not say to himself before a race, "I cannot do this. What if I trip? What if I fall?" No, instead Usain says: "I have no limits, everything is possible." Widely considered the greatest sprinter of all time, Usain has won gold medals in the 100-metre and 200-metre races in an unprecedented three straight Olympic Games.

There will always be those who criticize us, who will throw roadblocks and obstacles in our path to try and negate our dreams. But the only reason these naysayers do this is because they are of the mind that if they can't achieve their dreams, why should we be able to achieve ours? For if we are achieving our dreams, then others will have to take an inventory of their own goals to see why they are not achieving theirs. Looking inward can be a difficult and painful exercise. But when we focus on our own dreams and promises to ourselves, we are filled with the light of our intentions as we hold success at the tips of our fingers. The Dalai Lama said that when we cultivate sincere motivation, we will be successful.

The mind is our most powerful tool; all we have to do is decide what it is we want in life, and then unequivocally put all of our energy toward those markers. At the end of the day, imagination and action are more important than philosophical knowledge.

So how do we do this? How do we power our minds to actualize our life's goals, both materially and spiritually?

Well, the first step is to have a clear and calm mind, which is achievable through meditation. The practice of meditation quiets all the white noise in our head and allows us to listen to our heart's messages.

And as a part of this it is critical to accept and live life on life's terms. There are times when, inexplicably, we compare our lives to others who post only their most reimagined and aspirant lifestyles on social media. Couched in the human emotions of envy and jealously, we then question why this person seems to be so happy or how they can afford the time and money to take the exquisite vacations they are going on — all the while wondering why we aren't reveling in these same life situations. And so, rather than feeling blessed for what we have, we start to feel diminished, like what we have is not enough. What is important to remember in these situations is that many of the photos on social media platforms are posed and aspirational rather than real-life situations.

Of course, it is no secret that the grass often tends to be nowhere-near greener on the other side of the fence. Rather than count the blessings of others, I encourage you to focus your attention on your own blessings and be grateful for the life that you have. Every second that we spend time fantasizing about someone else's dream is time that we are taking away from our own.

I have a habit of listing the things that I am grateful for on a daily basis, and I open-heartedly celebrate the successes of others. Rather than envy other people's accomplishments, I use them as my motivation and my inspiration. When we adopt a positive attitude and approach to life, we break the cycle of negativity and create a stronger and more powerful mindset.

More often than not the pursuit of happiness, which should come from within, becomes instead about material possessions. For example, we might attach parameters to the state of our happiness. We may say, "I will be happy when I receive that promotion." "I will be happy when I can buy this," or I will be happy when I meet my life partner." However, when these milestones or achievements finally come about, we don't often experience the inner happiness that we expected and craved. We may look at the new position we've been promoted to in the company and realize that we are spending way too much time at work; or if we buy the sleek car of our dreams we may suddenly realize that the expenses associated with it are much higher than we expected. Or we may focus on other parts of our life that we feel are not "perfect" in our eyes. All of these examples are a type of impoverished thinking. The way to alleviate these traps is encompassed in a simple philosophy: we must learn to live life *with* happiness, not *for* happiness — that being in a state of happiness is the way to actualizing our goals.

To achieve a state of contentment we must, first and foremost, be grateful for all the people and the gifts in our lives. We must then have the faith to put forth our best efforts as we surrender the outcome to the Universe. Having faith in the Universe, or the Higher Power you believe in, allows all of us to accept that we are in exactly the right place and that we are exactly where we are meant to be. Once topped up with this faith, we are equipped with the tools and grace to put forth our best efforts toward achieving our dreams, knowing that the Universe will provide to us the best possible outcome for our path forward. If we are able to change our mindset in this way, we will feel a sense of deep happiness and a sense of peace within that will stay constant even as the tides of life shift.

When we are consistent in our meditation, the solutions to overcoming life's challenges present themselves from a clearer and more positive spirit, which in turn allows us to handle them with less worry, frustration and angst. Life's lessons are often disguised as obstacles, but with a positive mindset there is an inherent sense in our hearts that we will be provided with the best kind of solution, one we often haven't had the foresight to envision. The pain we experience, impossibly hard to deal with at the time, is often the life gift that we utilize to extend empathy and compassion to the people closest to us. It is life's challenging events that make us who we are today, our scars a testament to our bravery, character and inner spirit light.

We are all "very good at preparing to live, but not very good at living," as Thích Nhất Hạnh observed in *Peace is Every Step: The Path of Mindfulness in Everyday Life* (Random House, 1992). The only time for us to be alive and awake is right now, in the present moment, something that is all too easy to forget as we ponder the past and make our plans for the future.

In other words our path to serenity, peace and a sense of fulfilment within is as close as taking our next aware breath. When we allow ourselves to be present, we are allowing ourselves to live life with happiness and to live life with life.

Of course, like you, my life is not untouched by the daily challenges, upsets and tragedies that living life on life's terms presents, but as a result of my daily meditation practice, I now possess the clarity, light and peace of knowing I am in the right place doing the right thing — all of which is a direct result of my connection with the Universe, which has been fostered through my daily meditation practice.

In fact, the importance of connecting with the soul of the Universe is a concept celebrated by Paulo Coelho in *The Alchemist*, a book that has had a profound impact on my life. In his book, Coelho states that all things are connected to the soul of the Universe and that when we meditate we foster that connection.

"When we strive to become better than we are, everything around us becomes better, too," Coelho says.

When our hearts are connected to the soul of the Universe, and we are open to receiving its messages, we are more readily able and open to receiving the guidance we seek from above. Our hearts know the thoughts and emotions that we carry within and always whisper the ultimate truths to both our conscious and unconscious minds. The more we allow our heart to speak, and the more we heed what it has to say, the stronger our connection becomes.

My loved ones know that when they are going through difficult times I always ask them this heart-directed question: "How is your heart feeling about this situation, person or event?" More often than not, our minds tend to direct our paths. But when we listen and rely on our hearts for direction, I have found that I always receive the message, the advice that I need. As mentioned in Chapter 2, I have made it a habit to check in with my heart not just on a daily basis, but several times throughout the day, to make sure that it is satiated and serene and that I have not missed any of its important messages. This kind of practice is like a heart meditation, one that speaks in simple terms to our hearts. And if we make this process a consistent habit, it will make a difference in the ways that our hearts speak to us. I found that it also helps ensure that I am on the right path to pursuing my soul purpose, because it is our heart's light that illuminates our path. We are on this Earth for a reason and we each have our own exclusive purpose for being here. When we meditate and are in tune with the Universe, we are able to readily understand the steps we need to life live *with* happiness, rather than *for* happiness. These are gifts that allow us to celebrate the life that is uniquely crafted for each one of us.

At this juncture, I would like to share a little background around my initial meditation practice.

To be honest, when I first began meditating, I was not sure if I was even doing it right. I loved the feeling of not thinking about my day or about the pending tasks on my list. But I also loved the ability to let my mind wander. But as I mentioned in an earlier chapter, for the longest time I used what was supposed to be my meditation time to daydream. If you have tried to meditate but instead are inundated with a cascade of scenarios as to what happened the day before, what you need to plan next or even what happened to you that morning, that is OK. I encourage you not to be hard on yourself, for it is important to treat ourselves with love. Instead, let yourself recognize the jumbled thoughts that are crowding your mind and allow yourself a minute or two to let them dissipate into the air, telling yourself, "I can come back to my 'to do's later." When we speak to ourselves with a loving heart, we will notice a huge difference as we continue our sessions to clear our minds.

I am briefly going to outline, in a simple and easy manner, the steps to initiating a meditation practice. Know that meditating is a personal practice, and that one size does not fit all. So, if photographs of advanced yogis sitting cross-legged on hard wooden floors look intimidating and impossibly uncomfortable — just not something you imagine yourself doing — do not feel obligated to take that posture. Meditation is best done seated, can be cross-legged, against a wall or on a chair. So, find a position that best suits you, one in which you feel comfortable and does not create physical stress, which can become its own distraction.

Once you are in your comfortable position close your eyes, if possible. As you take a full breath in and a full breath out, acknowledge what is going on in your mind. If you are experiencing monkey mind, take another minute to inhale and exhale out your busy thoughts. Take another deep breath in, and this time allow the inhalation to completely fill your lungs and your belly. Slowly exhale and allow the breath to leave your body.

Take another breath and inhale deeply, and as you exhale, envision that all of your stress and any negative emotions, such as anger, stress or anxiety, are leaving your body. And now when you inhale, envision that you are filling your body with love, light and happiness. If at any time your mind starts to wander, simply bring it back to your breath.

Repeat these inhale and exhale exercises two to three more times.

Hopefully, you will notice that as you bring your awareness to your breath and as you inhale through the nose and exhale out the mouth, there is a natural relaxed flow. Also, as you bring your awareness to your breath, I ask that you notice the effects the breath is having on your body as a whole. Are your shoulders relaxed? Is your stomach slowly releasing its twisted knots of stress and anxiety?

When you are done with these exercises, put your hands together in the Namaste position as you thank your mind for this time of calming quiet and thank the Universe for this connecting experience.

Congratulations.

These simple breathing exercises represent your first venture into meditation practice.

Because I have been working with you on your breathing, I will briefly talk further about the practice of Pranayama. Prana represents our breath or life force, and yama speaks to control. As such, the practice of pranayama allows us to control our breathing in ways that are healing and beneficial to our bodies. Practicing Pranayama before meditating allows our minds to settle into a restful and still state, which in turn allows us to connect to our spirit as it cleanses our bodies of negativity and toxins.

I will also address here the chakras that make up our body. While it is not critical for the meditation newcomer to know these chakras on an intimate basis, it is information that can serve us well as we deepen our intentions and spiritual connections and move forward in our meditation practice.

"Chakras," a Sanskrit word taken from the classical language of India and Hinduism, means "wheels" or "disks," and refers to the energy and life centres in our bodies. The spiritual teachings of Dr. Sri Amit Ray tell us that there are 114 chakras within our being — two of which exist within our aura and 112 which exist within our body. These latter chakras are further divided into seven dimensions, which make up the seven chakras that we focus on in our meditation mindfulness and when we are practicing yoga. Interestingly, we can only work on 108 of the 112 chakras — the other four activate automatically.

Our seven energy centres are found along the spine, from the tail bone to the crown of our head. These energy centres are like lotus flowers that open and bloom as they grow toward the light of the Divine.

Within these energy centres, the seven chakras — root, sacral, solar plexus, heart, throat, eye and crown — open during our meditation practice. It is believed that the sounds that emanate from mantra chanting are instrumental in aligning the right and left hemispheres of our brains.

Chakras are energy sources that are located in the spinal column and run from the base of the spine to the crown of the head. The seven main chakras act as the conduits between our physical bodies and our collective consciousness.

And when we use the dual tools of breathing and chanting as we begin our meditation, our hearts will connect to the intentions of our spirits.

Colours are also a defining component of the seven chakras, with each one symbolizing its own unique purpose or power. In fact, the colour of one's energy field is often associated with the essential elements of one or several chakras.

The first, or *Root, Chakra* (known in Sanskrit as Muladhara Chakra), whose colour is red, is located at the base of the spine. As a "root" chakra, it represents grounding nourishing elements and has a connection with the earth's powerful energy source.

Its related sound is Lam.

Affirmations to manifest this chakra are:

I am grounded.

I am strong.

The second chakra, known as the *Sacral Chakra* (Sanskrit name: Swadhisthana), is connected with the colour orange. Believed to have unlimited and powerful energy, this chakra, whose sound is Vam, is located slightly above the base of the spine. It is associated with our emotions, creativity and moral values and is said to be where our egos reside.

Affirmations for this chakra:
I am free from my ego.
My ego does not drive me, but rather love.
I am exactly where I need to be.

The third chakra, or the *Solar Plexus* (Sanskrit name: Manipura Chakra), whose associated colour is yellow, and whose sound is Ram, represents our intelligence, confidence and personal power. This chakra is located just below the navel and is the centre of our emotions and is in fact where our self-esteem resides, nurturing us to be positive, loving and poised.

Affirmations for this chakra:
I am in control of my emotions.
I am feeling centred.
I am open to feeling and to expressing myself.

The fourth chakra, or *Heart Chakra* (Sanskrit name: Anahata), is centred in our chest. This chakra, whose colour is green and which has the sound Yam, fosters compassion within us. It is also connected to our ability to both love and love unconditionally with trust and a positive spirit as it flows throughout the seven chakra frequencies.

Affirmations:
I am free to love.
I am love.
My heart is open to love.
I love myself and I have love for others.

The fifth or *Throat Chakra* (Visuddha) facilitates communication and energy throughout the passageways of our body.

It is represented by the colour blue and is connected to our hearts, which allows us to freely express ourselves in a manner that emits love and positivity, both to others and to ourselves. Its sound is Ham.

Affirmations for this chakra:

I will use loving words toward myself and others.

I communicate freely and lovingly.

I express my feelings and communicate effectively.

The sixth chakra, the *Third Eye* (Sanskrit name: Ajna), whose colour is purple and which has the sound of Aum, is located between our eyebrows. This chakra is associated with intuition, which allows us to listen and respect the wisdom of our inner voices. The more that we are aware of the perceptions and guidance with which our intuition provides us, the more powerful is our Third Eye Chakra.

Affirmations for this chakra include:

I trust my intuition to guide me.

I hear my intuition and trust in its guidance.

I am intuitive, and I listen to my heart's guidance.

The seventh and last chakra is the *Crown Chakra* (Sanskrit name: Sahasrara), and it is located at the crown of our head. Its sound is the familiar Om.

Its white colour represents the synergy between our spirituality and our conscious being, and it is believed, in fact, to connect us with the Divine Universe.

Affirmations to manifest this chakra:

I am connected to the universe.

AUSPICIOUS

I am connected to a greater power.
I am surrounded by an aura of white light.

When our seven chakras are aligned, we have the power and opportunity to allow the divine light to fill our very beings.

When we are attuned to all seven of our chakras, our state of being is such that we feel grounded, positive, centred and at peace. However, when even one or two of these life-affirming elements are blocked, we tend to feel out of sorts, stressed, anxious and "not quite right." The good news is that through meditation we are able to reignite these energy centres which allows the seven chakra passageways to once again flow into each other and create a renewed sense of well-being.

In addition to these seven chakras, we have the ability to connect on a deeper level with our spirituality and intentions through the five elements contained within our five fingers, called mudras.

These five finger elements are: thumb, which contains the fire element; the index finger, whose element is air; the middle finger, whose element is space; the ring finger, which represents the earth element; and the pinky finger, which represents water.

To manifest the sacred, universal Gyan or mudra knowledge position we gently bring our thumb and index finger together in order to open the air element that is tied to enhanced spirituality.

All these important lessons that we take from meditating and connecting with our own Higher Powers are the realization that we need to live *with* happiness, not *for* happiness. That, indeed, each one of us has the power to change the meaning of "impossible" and redefine its intention so that we are affirmatively embracing "I am possible." In doing so, we make ourselves the heroines (and heroes) of our stories, not the victims or the villains.

As a means of facilitating and empowering our journeys, I am including some personal examples of meditations that I have created to use at or on specific times or days of the year.

Such as on January 1, when we collectively embark on the new calendar year, a time when we begin anew with the possibilities that lie ahead for us, I make it a point to acknowledge and reset my intentions for what is, rather than what was.

Meditation:

It is a new year, a time to reimagine a new you, with an abundance of new energy. Every day is as if we are born again.

Yesterday does not matter, and what is currently in front of us is what is possible, what can be.

No matter what regrets we might have, there is always new goodness and value to be created.

No matter how many opportunities have been lost or ignored, there is always more to be lived and fulfilled.

No matter what has been done with what was, we now have the ability to become what is possible. We have endless possibilities to build and actualize our intentions in the best ways we can ever imagine.

It all starts within; it all starts today.

As I dedicate myself to this New Year, I commit to letting go of all negative feelings: anger, regret, jealousy, envy, sadness, fear and ego. I resolve to begin this year with a clean slate, opening myself up to love, opportunity, compassion, happiness and confidence.

The Universe conspires to help each one of us achieve our soul purpose, which as you well know now is defined for me by the three simple but powerful words that you have seen repeated several times throughout this book: *Courage, Conviction and Confidence.*

When we are kind to and with ourselves, we are speaking the language of love with self-directed gentleness, empathy and light. We throw away old behaviours and ways of talking to ourselves such as calling ourselves fat or criticizing how we look or how we feel we might not fit in. These kinds of self-recriminations no longer hold any weight. In fact, in a bizarre twist on human behaviour, if a friend said the things to us that we say to ourselves — things like we're fat, we don't look good in a particular jacket or outfit, our hips are too big, our hair is too thin — it is guaranteed that we would no longer be friends with that person, let alone be their soulmate. And isn't that what we should strive to be for and with ourselves? Soulmates with a soul purpose?

So, what does changed behaviour look like — what and who do we want to envision as we sit in meditation and do the work to connect to our soul purpose?

To begin, I highly recommend that we each take the time to look in the mirror and embrace ourselves, warts and all. I suggest then getting paper and pen and writing down a list of all the traits that we love and admire about ourselves. We need to be rigorously honest and embrace our individual God-given talents. This is not an exercise born out of ego, but rather one centred in self-love. If there are traits that need to be worked on, that you think could use some honest and valid improvement, write them down as well and embrace them with self-respect, courage and intent. There is absolutely no benefit in being our own worst enemies, the bully in our own sandbox.

Having confidence in our own abilities to move forward with absolute conviction sparks happiness from within which, in turn, creates positive energy. Each one of us has the singular ability to shine like the brightest of lights on a clear, cold night. We have the fire within. We just need to discover how to ignite it.

So just how do we do that?

We begin by having the courage to sit in silence and connect, in meditation, to the God, Higher Power or deity that we personally believe in, which, in fact, is the Universe's guiding light.

Dr. Martin Luther King Jr. said it best: "Darkness cannot drive out darkness; only light can do that. Hate cannot drive out hate;

only love can do that."

In other words, good will come to us when we choose to live *with* happiness, not *for* happiness.

By choosing to explore a path of meditation, you have already taken a first step toward happiness by giving yourself an opportunity to listen to your heart, which always speaks the truth.

But there needs to be an awareness of how we can build the kind of strength and faith that allows us to get back up when we fail, when we fall.

As the Japanese proverb famously says: "Fall down seven times, get up eight."

It is faith in ourselves and our abilities, both of which we source and connect with as we sit in meditation, that make us stronger within ourselves and against outside forces.

Without a doubt, we all experience difficult times and often feel like we are being tested, chosen by the Universe to endure the kinds of challenges that we think others are not experiencing. It is my personal belief, as I have stated previously, that God is not in the business of testing us. Rather, He puts challenges in front of us as a testament to His belief in each one of us as we go about discovering our Soul Purpose in life. Difficult times, no matter in what arena of our lives, allow us to strengthen our faith — both in ourselves and in the Higher Being of our choice, however that presents itself to us personally — because He knows that by giving us our free will to resolve and conquer our fears and issues, we find the strength to evolve and actualize our more authentic selves as loving human beings.

Fear, a topic which I have spoken about on more than one occasion in this book, is an emotion that we have all experienced in our lives, one that is more often than not merely based on false, fabricated thoughts we conjure without any fact-based evidence.

As the wise old adage by U.S. president Franklin D. Roosevelt states: "The only thing we have to fear is ... fear itself."

In other words, and in the context of overcoming our negative thoughts and anxieties, in order to achieve the traits and personal goals that we aspire to, the only thing we should fear is fear.

When we sit in meditation and connect with the silence and the power within our breaths, we build our sense of courage and self-esteem which, in turn, quiets the internal fears of not being worthy enough to be a part of the Universe's greater plan. Our inner strength does not come from what we can do, but from overcoming the things we once thought we could not do.

And so, it is important to understand that fear is a double-sided coin with opposite intentions. We have the conscious choice to either fear everything and run — or face everything and rise above. Courage does not always present itself as a roaring voice but rather as that quiet whisper at the end of the day that says, "I will try again tomorrow." We never know how strong we are until strength is the only choice we have.

The goodness of what can be is far more powerful than any memory of what has been. We must embrace this thought fully. Now is the time when we can turn what can be into what is. Positive possibilities are available to all of us, no matter what may have happened previously.

The metamorphosis of a caterpillar into a butterfly is an apt metaphor for our challenging life experiences, a time when we evolve out of the darkness and into the light.

It is important to understand and accept that God chooses us to go through the struggles that we do because He has faith in us. It is important to believe that the challenges that we experience are blessings in disguise, because within them lie the lessons in life that make us stronger and ever more resilient. Happiness is found in the moment that we are able to let go of what we cannot change — a conscious decision that takes strength and courage.

As the popular Serenity Prayer states: "God give me the courage to accept the things that I cannot change, courage to change the things I can, and the wisdom to know the difference."

The willingness and courage to accept our lack of power or helplessness toward a given person or circumstance is the first step toward the grace and serenity that comes from acceptance.

The following is a meditation that I use to deepen and embrace acceptance:

I AM.
Accepting myself means accepting all of me.
I have confidence and conviction in all of my abilities.
I have the courage to raise my inner voice higher than the noise of the criticism that surrounds me.
I tell myself I am. I can.
I am beautiful.
I am strong.
I look in the mirror and I accept my flaws, while also acknowledging my inner and outer beauty.
I am sincere.
I am confident.
I AM.
I CAN.
I WILL.

The Dalai Lama teaches us: "A calm mind brings inner strength, and inner strength brings inner happiness."

It is a teaching that inspires the valuable decision to become an affirmative warrior rather than a full-time worrier. Indeed, it is this kind of daily intention that is worth adopting as part of the mosaic of our daily meditation practice.

The practice of visualization — who we want to be, what we want to achieve, how we want to feel — is a proven strategy used by athletes who want to build their strengths, overcome their fears, and better their overall competitive outcomes. Everyone from Olympic coaches to NHL teams to NBA players have used strategic visualization techniques to build not just physical strength but mental and emotional fortitude, toughness and resilience. We can use this practice of visualization in our personal meditation practice as well, for it is within our open and resting subconscious that our subliminal messages seed and flourish, sprouting from deeply entrenched roots to emerge from our unconscious state of being to a conscious sense of purpose which, in turn, allows us to grow toward a state of true enlightenment.

What can be begins in this moment. What can be comes from our thoughts, our actions and the discipline, passion and commitment with which we live from this point forward.

When we bloom where we're planted, wherever that may be, the results that we hope for will manifest themselves in the living light of love, faith and hope.

CHAPTER 9

THE DIVINE FEMININE: CELEBRATING OUR EMPOWERED, CREATIVE INNER GODDESSES

"Woman is a ray of God. She is not that earthly beloved: she is creative, not created."

— Rumi

As I introduce you to my most joyous and intuitive connection with my own personal Divine Feminine, I promise you that there is no need for you to run for the hills. I am not about to launch into a "woo-woo" dissertation of new-age jargon.

I completely understand that some of you may think that the term "Divine Feminine" is a catchphrase that opens the door to all things witchery and spells, or maybe even to a feminist rant.

I assure you that this is not the case.

Rather, I have specifically chosen this chapter, Chapter 9 — which celebrates our empowered, creative inner Goddesses — to be the last chapter in this book because the number 9, which in my Hindu culture signifies selflessness, humanitarianism and spiritual awareness, is an auspicious place for me to conclude.

The number 9 is also understood to signify wisdom and experience, while also symbolizing the awakening and inner wisdom garnered through our life experiences and struggles.

We additionally have nine Devis, or Goddesses, who represent a variety of auspicious attributes, such as power, strength, divinity, courage, devotion, patience, knowledge, health, prosperity, peace, power, success and fulfilment. And it is my creative inner Goddesses that allow me to passionately pursue my soul purpose on a consistent basis.

And so you see, the number 9, as it relates to the Divine Feminine, is an auspicious number indeed.

In Hinduism we have many Goddesses, who represent different aspects of life. Moreover, there are Goddesses associated with each chakra. What is interesting to note is that within Hinduism all our male Gods are depicted in such a way that they portray traditionally female characteristics. This is because Hinduism teaches that each person has male and female energies and they work together in unison to create a unique individual.

Pingala Nadi, which runs along our body's right side, is actually preeminent in the left side of our brain. Masculine and methodical, it is responsible for keeping us organized and logical.

Ida Nadi, which is preeminent in the right side of our brain, runs along our body's left side. Responsible for our passion, imagination and our sensuality, it represents our feminine creative side.

As such, it is the two-sided traits of Pingala Nadi and Ida Nadi that allow both our masculine and feminine sides to live in harmony with one another. As society has moved from a system that was patriarchal to one that reflects much deeper feminine attributes and values, our masculine and feminine selves are drawing closer in our shared experiences and our conjoined efforts.

The number 9 is also significant as it is said that there are nine heavenly bodies and deities, all of whom have an effect on human life. They include the sun (Surya), moon (Chandra), Mars (Mangala), Mercury (Buddha), Jupiter (Brihaspati), Venus

(Shukra), Saturn (Shani), Rahu (the moon's north nodule) and Ketu (the moon's south protuberance).

So what exactly does the term "the Divine Feminine" mean?

Urban Dictionary describes the Divine Feminine as "a woman who is unapologetically herself." Intuitive and full of love, such a woman is one with the Universe and God and embraces the beauty of nature. She owns her voice and can speak her truth fearlessly, not depending on external factors to prove her worth, which she intuitively knows she embodies.

For me, the essence of the Divine Feminine encompasses my empowered creative inner goddesses as a means to setting the world ablaze with the fire of love, for love is not just in our hearts and it is not just in one person. Rather, love is in everything that the sun nourishes with warmth and light. It is in everything that the moon illuminates. It is everyone and everything created by God. It is the energy that binds us all together and allows me — and you — to achieve our dreams, to be ourselves and to act selflessly to better ourselves by lifting others up. It is also about showing our compassion and empathy and our intuition and connection with Nature, while fostering healing practices and nurturing words and actions.

These are all principles of the Divine Feminine, the love that is spoken to us through the Universe.

My Divine Feminine is also my spiritual lens, one that, as a living practice, allows me to live my life with kindness, courage, conviction and confidence, with a mind frame that, at all times, inspires and guides me as to how I, Reetu Gupta, can make an impactful difference on others' lives.

As well, within my daily meditation practices, both on a personal basis and in the classes I teach, I listen to, connect and accept the Universe's guidance and answers to my prayers. I make it a point to support everyone, both women and men, with whom I come in contact throughout my day. Importantly, I do my utmost on a continuous basis to live my life without fear or ego.

In truth, it is a manifestation of selfless love, built on the feminine virtues of gratitude and spirituality, all of which are grounded and connected in mindfulness, prayer and meditation.

And so, whether it was my fledgling intuition or my personal Goddess that facilitated my being born on January 13th, which is when Lohri, the only holiday in the Hindu culture that does not follow the lunar calendar and falls on the same date every year, is celebrated, I consider my arrival on that January day a most auspicious start to my life.

Lohri is special because it celebrates the start of a new harvest and the start of longer days. The festival includes such rituals as having bonfires and eating all kinds of wonderful foods. It is believed that the Goddess of Lohri is married to the Fire God and that together on this day they bring about a fruitful harvest with promises of an opportune season ahead.

So being born on this day has always been a sign to me from the Universe that my life's path was destined to be *auspicious and unique.*

It will come as no surprise to you, then, that my favourite number — 13, my birth date — is the number said to embody the Divine Feminine and, for me, represents magic, mystery and curiosity.

I thoroughly enjoy immersing myself in my Hindu culture and, as a part of that, I love to reflect and celebrate the many Goddesses that are an integral part of our beliefs.

The Goddess that I personally connect with, love and admire is Radha, who is the twin flame of Krishna. She embodies pure divine love, and her love for Krishna in particular is so pure that legend has it that if you pray to Radha, you will receive Krishna's richest blessings. It is said that Radha's love is so pure that if a devotee loves her, they will also garner Krishna's love and protection.

Of course, there are other Goddesses that light my way, including Goddess Lalita, who reminds me that life is meant to be happy, that we should always strive to embrace a childlike state of play, and we should always be mindful of the importance of smiles and laughter.

There is also Goddess Parvati, who represents strength, or Shakti. She is a warrior and is deeply devoted to her twin flame, Lord Shiva.

It is my connection with these Goddesses that allows and inspires me to make the decisions that best fit my situations at hand.

This is important because we, especially as women, are often pressured to be all things to all people. We are expected to perform multiple roles on a daily basis. Society expects us to morph ourselves into a form that is traditional and acceptable, which means we have to downplay our own wants and needs.

But then there are those like me, wild ones, daring ones, who make the unequivocally brave decision to refuse to change the makeup of our souls for society's sake.

Rather, we push forward, wild, free and unfettered. This is my wish for you.

And the truth is, we all feel the call of the wild spirit within us, which I consider to be the voice of the Divine Feminine, the voice that guides me on a trusted intuitive basis.

Author Clarissa Pinkola Estés, Ph.D., suggests in her book *Women Who Run with the Wolves: Myths and Stories of the Wild Woman Archetype* (Ballantine Books, 1992) that every woman possesses powerful sources of knowledge, creativity and intuition within herself. She also suggests that within every woman "there is a wild and natural creature, a powerful force, filled with good instincts, passionate creativity and ageless knowing."

She argues that even though we each started out as Wild Women, our free spirits have been tamed by society's rules and perceptions, limiting our fire and purpose.

This begs the question: Why should a woman's ambition and thinking be limited? Why is there a need for statistics about the number of women who hold powerful leadership roles in the Top Fortune 500 Companies, for instance? Why does it feel like there are still limits on what women can achieve? Why does our society do this to women?

I am fairly confident that no one has ever told NBA basketball legend LeBron James to stop scoring and give someone else a chance. No one ever points out that he is a male basketball player. It is just a given.

So why isn't it the accepted norm for women to hold powerful CEO positions or to be inducted into elite male-bastion establishments such as the Hockey Hall of Fame?

I've walked into many a boardroom filled with men and I've seen the doubt, the smirks on their faces. Ah, the "female" CEO, their body language projects, as if they think I don't belong. I have been in situations where men purposely speak three decibels higher than me just to drown out my voice, trying to intimidate me.

It has been often said that if we don't believe in anything, we will fall for anything. I believe this is true, and because of my faith and my belief in myself I feel protected and whole.

Interestingly, too, when a man speaks up for women's rights, he is brave — a protector and a defender.

But when a woman has the courage to stand up and speak for women's rights, to speak up against discrimination and racism, society reacts in a fearful way. Sadly, there are people who feel intimidated and, because of that fear, they campaign against an outspoken woman's power and confidence, ultimately using her courage to malign her. Yes, I am strong, and yes, I will always speak up with the intention of uplifting humanity. I love all humankind, and I will do whatever it takes to bring equality and love into the world. If that's what it takes to change racist thinking and the poor treatment of women, so be it.

And I don't really understand the term "woman of colour."

Why does this term make it seem as though people whose skin isn't white are abnormal? Personally, I don't like this term. Rather, I prefer to say I am a woman *with* colour: I am all sorts of shades of gold, and I shine with the light of my inner intentions, confidence and unwavering gratitude for the gifts in my life every single day.

I love being underestimated because my fire, my strength and my intelligence surprises people. My words are not meant as a criticism against any specific cohort; rather it is my mandate, my Divine Feminine, urging you to not let any person take away your voice or your inner power.

In *The Art of War*, Sun Tzu says, "He will win who knows when to fight and when not to fight."

For me, this means lead by listening, not by talking. It is my intuitive heart and the guidance from my connection with my Divine Feminine that powers me forward through difficult situations.

In fact, it is my connection with my Divine Feminine that has allowed me to manifest my most authentic self from the time I was quite young.

Throughout my life, I have had many people offer me unsolicited advice about the things I should do, how I should dress, what I should say — or not say.

When I was younger, I was told that I was too strong, too loud, too powerful, and that I would be too much for a man to handle.

I found this very confusing at times because as I looked around me, I saw young men who were around the same age as me, acting in the same ways. I saw no one telling them that they needed to trim their spirits or their very beings. Absolutely no one was telling them that they were "too much." I was hurt and discouraged by the inequality of it all. Why did I have to be the one who needed to change in order to fit into someone else's perceptions of how I should be?

That being said, I did not have, nor do I have now, any desire to change who I am.

I have never wanted to be like someone else; I have always celebrated who I am. I want to be me — the one who laughs uncontrollably by herself, who talks too fast, who has boundless energy and ideas, many of which are successful not only financially but also as charitable advocacy. The last thing that I want is to trade in my authenticity, my singular connection with my Divine Feminine, to take on someone else's persona.

Why?

Because I am confident there is a path that has been created for me by the Divine Universe, one that is meant specifically for me. I was put on this earth for a purpose, and the way that I can best achieve this purpose is to just be myself.

As I have mentioned previously, I love fashion, and I use it as a means to express myself. My choice of clothing and jewelry communicate, on any given day, my energy, my purpose and my light.

For me, fashion is art. I am always wearing at least three colourful chains as well as bangles and earrings, all of which hold deep spiritual meaning for me. Growing up, I heard "Reetu, are you sure you want to wear that? It's a lot. It's too clunky," or "it's too colourful" so many times. Or "Are you going to work dressed like *that*? Aren't those earrings too big to wear to work?" However, I have always had one rule in my life, a yardstick that I continue to live by, which is that I will not let anyone or anything compromise my integrity. This is who I am. I have my own set of standards for myself and, as a result, I never feel the need to defend my decisions. Why?

Because I have faith in myself and my decision-making. I know in my heart what is right, and I do not feel the need to prove my worth to anyone. I trust my affirming spirit and my belief in my Divine Feminine purpose. It is in this place that I thrive.

As I have stated many times throughout this book, it is the struggles that we go through, and what we do to resolve them, that nurture and inspire us to fulfil our own specific purpose in life.

Maybe your struggle has been one of ascertaining your identity or of wanting to fit in, of wanting to be accepted. However, if you choose to live your life as others want you to, if you choose to imitate others rather than be yourself, you will not be free to actualize your most authentic, auspicious self. Your heart will not be happy in the long run because your soul is aching to fulfil your own personal destiny. It's when we are authentically ourselves that our true energy is found and where our light shines the brightest. It is when we make the decision to live life as our best selves that we honour our heart. We put our trust and faith in the Universe and our hand in the Divine Feminine so that we can walk the path of our soul purpose with light and delight.

When we are able to live in this authentic energy, we are then free-spirited enough to live in the aura of true happiness. I would much rather go through life knowing that I did it my way, that I've been true to myself, as opposed to living my life in a way that others dictated.

We are all accountable for our own possibilities in life, and although we might not all be gifted with the talents and capabilities we had hoped for, we have been gifted with the intuition that allows us to connect with our purposeful Divine Feminine.

Whatever we need to become who we would like to be already exists within us. We are worthy of the life we desire. We are capable of achieving our dreams. I encourage you to have faith and hope in the fact that we all deserve happiness and fulfilment in our everyday lives despite the challenges that we may be going through.

It is all about blessing our struggles.

Another question that I often get is, "Where do you get your confidence from?" It is not something that I really thought about until I sat down to write this book, to be truthful.

I am blessed with a family and a circle of friends who have always supported me. My parents taught me to be confident and self-assured in both a physical and emotional way. When I was young, they would tell me to hold my head up, to believe in myself no matter what, and to believe in my ideas and my ideals. As I rose through the ranks at my family's company, having first served in a variety of positions from the ground up, my dad would always tell me, "Don't be shy, speak up in meetings, voice your ideas and let everyone hear you."

My mom always supported my sense of fashion and my vocal advocacy for those less fortunate, for those who were being picked on or discriminated against. My brother, Suraj, has continuously supported all of my different business ideas; in fact, he is my confidant and my rock. I am blessed to have strong and affirming connections with my sisters, both with those who are related to me by blood and to my kindred-heart sisters, for having sisters means that I have women that I know I can count on no matter what, to be with me, laugh with me, cry with me, shop with me. My sisters are intuitive; they know without being asked when I need their love and support. It is this bond that is irreplaceable, mystifying in the best possible way.

It is these relationships that I have created and fostered with my familial siblings and my heart siblings that have given me the great heart to walk the path of my soul purpose with courage, conviction and confidence.

My confidence also comes from my faith in God. I find peace and strength and courage in my faith, all of which allow me to have conviction and confidence in every step that I take.

I have found that the key to connecting with my Divine Feminine is to surround myself with women who are there to support and elevate me, who will pray for me and celebrate me, rather than talk against me or behind my back.

As women, we should not feel that we need to fit into an idea or mould that society has created for us. We do not need to follow a set of regulations that are long outdated and, truthfully, should not have been in place to begin with.

Why exactly were women refused the right to vote until they rose up in protest? Why were women who got married in the 1950s no longer allowed to work?

I could compile an endless list of examples of women's disempowerment, situations that no longer exist because of the vocal advocacy of women who are powerful examples in all of our lives. Women such as former First Lady Michelle Obama, whose "Let's Move" initiative helped to fight child obesity; Nobel Laureate Malala Yousafzai, who fought for girls to be allowed to go to school; champion tennis star Serena Williams, who continues to advocate for social change; Tarana Burke, civil rights activist and the founder of the #METOO movement; and singer and philanthropist Beyoncé, who epitomizes the tenets of the Divine Feminine. These are just a handful of the women that I respect as change leaders and authentic models, ones who truly actualize the concept of the Divine Feminine in both their personal lives and on the global stage.

Those of us who are connected to our Divine Feminine are creators and nurturers and advocates with the energy that allows us to be powerful, protective and loving. And so it is important to note that the Divine Feminine is not reserved just for those who identify as women. Each one of us has masculine and feminine traits, and we each have the ability to harness the beauty, the magic and the power of the Divine Feminine.

Trust in your heart, for it is that pulsating energy that intuitively guides our paths. I am sure that you have, as I have, personally experienced the irony that when matters of the heart are concerned, reason and logic are oftentimes absent. I have found that where there is love, there needs to be no reason. I have also found that the most exciting things that have happened in my life happened in the moments when I was following my heart. This is where we find the magic in life; in the heart' centre of our soul.

And so, my wish for you is that you allow your extraordinary light to illuminate your soul purpose, and that as we act as a cohort that is *inclusive* rather than exclusive, together, we will light up the world with tolerance and possibilities and make it a more loving, peaceful place.

In doing so, I implore you to always stay curious because curiosity is what breathes life into our dreams and joy and magic into our lives.

When we believe in magic, the Universe shines with the delight of knowing that we are doing our utmost to actualize and manifest our destinies.

And as a part of that, and in recognition of our efforts, the Universe is happy to bestow its magical stardust of dream-catchers and dream accomplishments on those of us who believe. It is the Universe's way of gifting us with hugs of gratitude for honouring the principles that are inherent within the essence of the Divine Feminine, and also for honouring the very reason we are on this Earth — to actualize the dreams within our heart. This is ultimately the common denominator on all our paths, inspiring us all to live life with a glad heart and a magnificently joyous spirit.

As we close this chapter of the journey that we have been on together throughout the pages of this book, I leave you with some final thoughts on what living a Divine Feminine life means to me.

It is having the free spirit and grace that allows me to live life with courage, conviction and unconditional love for my fellow human beings.

It is living life with an attitude of gratitude and adopting habits and disciplines that are life-affirming. By committing to consistent meditation, which in turn gives me the tools to truly believe in myself, I am able to actualize my dreams, bless my struggles and celebrate my empowered creative goddesses.

Living a Divine Feminine life also means dancing with the joy of being my most authentic, auspicious self, something that I wish and pray for each one of you. It means celebrating our state of being, whether we are young and just setting out on our paths or elderly and already full of wisdom and experience.

We are all the authors — the writers — of our own life stories. Make sure that your beginnings, middles and endings flourish with the magic of the Divine Feminine's light. Make sure that you write yourself in as the heroine or hero of your own story.

As you embrace and celebrate your soul purpose in life, be courageous, be confident and live with conviction.

It is then that you will know the true meaning of living your most auspicious, authentic Divine Feminine purpose. When we celebrate our empowered creative inner Goddesses, we hold in our hands the opportunity to be advocates for and initiators of joy, peace, light and positivity in all the lives that we touch.

Be Daring.
Be Curious.
Be Love.

Dream Deeply,
Dream Curiously,
Love Deeply,
and *always* Love Unconditionally.